I0373834

PUBLISHED by PARABLES
Earthly Stories with a Heavenly Meaning

A Novel

COPPERLINE

By

Peter Michael Talbot

PUBLISHED by PARABLES

Earthly Stories with a Heavenly Meaning

COPPERLINE
Peter Michael Talbot

Published By Parables
October, 2019

ISBN 978-1-951497-05-7
Printed in the United States of America

A Novel

COPPERLINE

By

Peter Michael Talbot

PUBLISHED by PARABLES
Earthly Stories with a Heavenly Meaning

Dedicated to Beth.
A woman who has believed in
every crazy, ambitious idea I've ever had.
I love you.

Everything that you read in this account is true.

-Daniel Waters

PART ONE

One

I'm in so much trouble.

Dead.

If they find me this time, they'll kill me. They're going to rip me limb from limb.

I was running. I cursed with every step. I questioned myself. *Should I have stayed? This better be worth it. I have to make this time count.*

With every knee-jarring lunge, I gasped for more air. I escaped from the Specimen Dormitory and was running like hell.

I remembered the last time I tried this, I didn't get nearly as far as I did today. The guards threatened to kill me if I tried this stunt again. I just couldn't be contained in that prison one more day. *I wont!*

I dashed past several buildings, through only back allies. I had to get to the tree-line that surrounds the city. I heard the stories and rumors by other specs, just like me, going to a spot in the forest line where I could hide. There had been dozens that have tried to escape. Some were caught and returned , but others never made it back. *They probably killed them, like they're going to kill me.*

I kept sprinting, continuously turning my head back to see if the guards were closing in. I did my best to move quickly on stagnant legs. On a cloth, a friend drew for me a map to make it out of the downtown sector. None of this looked familiar. I held my makeshift map tightly in my right hand, examining it every few minutes. The hospital was located almost in the middle of the city. They grew a row of trees almost around the entire city, just in front of the wall. The faux forest was my desired destination.

I saw a handful of people, but none of them looked familiar. I watched as their eyes widened with curiosity as a man in a brown hospital gown moved past them frantically. I couldn't see the guards behind me, but I knew Copperline's finest would be on my trail like a pack of bloodhounds.

Trees. I think I made it. There was mention of a creek just beyond the treeline. The concrete buildings and pavement would soon turn into red pines and mossy ground. *Just one more jump to freedom. I'll buy time until I can figure my way out of this god-forsaken city.* I had to find shelter to hide from them and take a night to camp out. The next day, I'd wait for the delivery truck that comes once a week and jump in the back of the trailer. That fifty-three foot trailer would have to be my home for the few hundred miles. That was the best plan I could come up with. It was my only plan.

I've read books of people living like vagabonds, going from city to city, at the mercy of various forms of transportation. That sounded amazing compared to what I've had to live through at the spec dorm. I was hell bent not to take one more syringe of the poison they fill our veins with.

Once I got to the forest entrance, I noticed the creek ahead of me. I aimed my body and jumped with everything that I had. I used my momentum to project my entire frame forward. I cleared the creek with a foot and a half to spare, but I dropped my napkin map in the stream. The mossy covering felt cool and damp under my fingers as I landed and rolled forward.

I quickly surveyed of the area to determine where I should hide, but the covering was few and far between. *Come on. Think, spec. Think. Where can I go where they won't see me?*

I saw a tree that had been knocked down with the roots hanging high in the air. *There,* I thought. *I could hide there, at least until the guards give up and head back.*

I knew they wouldn't be satisfied knowing that I was somewhere out here in the woods, so they'd undoubtedly search again tomorrow with more guards. Of course, I was probably naive, but I had to find a spot for tonight and move accordingly.

Two more leaps forward and I would be in the clear. I took one more look back, but I didn't see or hear anybody. *I must've outrun them,* I figured. The guards are restrained within the city walls all day. I imagined that the only exercise they got was from walking their guard dogs.

"No!" *The dogs. How could I be so stupid? How could I forget about the dogs? They'll surely catch my scent and find me.*

I took off my outer clothes and threw them in the creek. I knew they would give off my scent, I had to get rid of them. I started dry-heaving as the anxiety running through my body was making me sick. I bent over and started coughing up mucous. I spit some vomit from my mouth as I continued to retch with my hands on my knees. I felt my back arch up as my chest and stomach violently contracted, trying to force me to puke.

Out of the corner of my eye, I spotted a muddy moss patch. I figured that if I was to survive against the dogs, my only hope is to mask my scent, so I began to roll around in the mud like I was some possessed pig man.

As I covered myself with the muck and mire, I noticed a flash of bright white coming from the base of the knocked-over tree. I didn't realize how far I had moved past my safe haven in my effort to mask my scent.

Catching myself staring at the tree, I realized I didn't have enough time for a game of 'I spy.' I frantically continued to pad myself with the musky smell of the fresh earth.

"Spec! Spec!" I heard the loud, throaty voice of a guard. *They caught up to me.* I wondered how long the guard had been there, watching me. For a slight moment, we made eye contact. I could see his perfectly formed frown. He slowly shook his head. He casually moved one foot in front of the other as if he was trying not to spook me with any sudden movements.

I had nowhere to go. I had no knowledge of the city outside the walls of the spec dorm. *I'm dead,* I thought to myself again.

Then a terrifying noise chilled me to my core: the sound of barking dogs. I looked to my left, but I didn't see them yet.

Shaking with rage, I screamed, "I'm not going back! I'm not going to be tortured anymore!"

I stood there in just my underwear which was now soaked in mud and moss. *Come on, move spec!* My own indecisiveness was like quicksand, paralyzing me.

"Just calm down, kid. You're better with us alive, than dead out here in the woods." Officer X128 shouted. He was a large and terrible man, just slightly older than myself. Now closing in on 50 meters, he could clearly see who I was. I recognized his dark skin and muscular build.

I was well acquainted with X128. The youngest of the guards, a lot of the specs referred to him as only X. He was also a spec at one time, but he was chosen to become a guard.

Why him? He's going to murder me.

There's no way out.

My heart was pounding out of my chest, but not all from the adrenaline and hype of the chase. I was angry at myself. I told myself that morning, this would be the day that I would escape and taste sweet sweet freedom. My dormmates told me I was insane for trying, but I couldn't take one more day of vaccine trials. Call it intuition. Call it a gut feeling, but today was the day.

Why can't I move? Where do I go? I was indignant with my immobility.

"Spec's over here!" X128 motioned to his other officers. One of the officers was holding back two leashed K-9s that looked like they were ready to have me for lunch. "It's not going anywhere!" He laughed, trying to intimidate me.

It. The guards always referred to us as "it," making us feel like animals. Hearing those words deflated me. I was running out of hope. I was questioning whether or not I really could escape.

Should I give up? No! Come on, spec! Move! Move!

"Give it up, kid! You're pathetic! I told you, you'll die out here in the woods. And if the woods don't kill you, I will. I'm sure the mayor won't miss one more ignorant spec," sneered X128. He was the worst. When the guards catch you, they make you pay for trying to escape, especially X, who had perfected the art of torture.

I looked around once more. I was running out of time and options. Then I saw it again, the flash of white coming from the base of the tree. *Is it a flag? A shirt? I think someone's over there.*

X took another step toward me, ranting and cursing as he trudged forward through the brush. I couldn't make out what he was saying as I was much too curious about what I was witnessing at the tree.

Then I clearly saw it. A hand stretching through the roots, was motioning me to come towards the tree that was between X and me. *Who is that? Friend? Foe?* I didn't have many options. Either I go back with X to be tortured, or take a risk by following an unidentified person waving from a base of an overturned tree. I didn't have to time mull this over in my head. A spark of hope was ignited. *I'm not going back to the hospital.* Too many failed escape plans that only led to serious beatings and extra doses of truth serum cluttered my past. I had enough.

I knew the guards couldn't see the arm motioning me as the tree was splitting the space between us. I heard a twig snap under X's boot. The sound was somehow amplified in my head. It was like a gun had been shot at the starting line of a marathon. I jolted into a sprint.

As soon as I started for the tree, a certain fear fell upon X's face. He looked at the tree, and then at me. It was almost as if he knew that I had found my way out. *He's been here before, hasn't he? Run, spec. Run!*

As he moved faster, X struggled over downed limbs and brush. "Dogs! Release the dogs!" He yelled. The officer holding the dogs released them on X's command. It seemed like they were moving at warp-speed and I was caught in slow motion.

No, no, no! Run!

Pain filled my lungs again. All the running, all the anxiety was getting to me.

The dogs flew over the obstacles. Eating up the ground, swallowing the distance between us.

Running. Tripping over my own feet. Trying to keep my balance.

Barking, and moving ever so swiftly through the woods, the dogs were so fast. Too fast.

I started to mutter as I ran, "no, no, no." Panic sent chills all over my body as I ran. My legs burned as I ran through painful cramps. My heart pounded in my chest. The phlegm in my mouth tasted metallic as I spit it to the ground. The sweat from my brow stung my eyes.

The arm began waving wildly before it disappeared into the dark roots at the base of the tree. I didn't even see a way in. *What do I do when I get there? What the hell?*

Before I even realized it, the dogs had passed X by several lengths and were only 10 meters away from the tree. I had little hope of making it. *Should I give up*, I asked myself. *They'll kill me if I do.*

A sharp pain in my knee. It felt as if one of the tendons on the outside of my leg tightened up, forcing me into a pathetic half-limp, half-jog. I let out a cry from the pain. *Just run through the pain, spec! Run!*

The dogs were bearing down and closing in. They jumped the creek with no problem at all. I aimed for where the arm was protruding. I dove for the tree crashing into cold, hard roots. I felt the rough surface of old wood cutting into my face. The wood from the roots cut into my neck, arms, and chest. Something sharp caught my ear so badly that I was certain I lost it. I cursed and screamed as a result of the pain.

There I was, flying into the roots of a tree. Instead of landing into a hard wooden surface, it felt as if I was falling down stone stairs. The warm Copperline air quickly turned cold and damp. The noontime sun disappeared.

I felt ribs crack. More screaming as a result of the pain. I was certain that I was falling down stairs, but was unsure where they were taking me.

Suddenly my body came to an abrupt stop. The air in my lungs was stolen from me. I gasped for breath. I laid there in such anguish. I moaned as I struggled to inhale.

I could hear the faint sound of the dogs wheezing and barking, but something prevented them from following me. Maybe they didn't see where I had disappeared.

After a few seconds, their barking stopped. The officer must've made it to the dogs and silenced them. I waited to hear the sound of X128, but heard nothing. *Did I make it? Why aren't they coming after me? Surely X will come after me,* I thought. I waited there for the sound of him rushing down the steps from which I fell, but nothing. No sound. A strange silence. Only broken by the pathetic sound of my labored breathing.

The room filled with some sort of reverse echo. I didn't know how to explain it. When I coughed, it echoed through the air, but almost as if the sound came repeated to me backward. The space had a thick and damp feel about it. It smelled of sulfur or rotten eggs. It was completely dark.

I started to feel around my body for cuts and bruises. I was sure that I had broken at least one of my ribs in the fall. It hurt to inhale so my short, labored breaths offered no real oxygen intake. However, shallow breaths were fine since the air was so rancid. *A broken gas line? What is that smell?* I asked myself.

Then I remembered why I was there in the first place. *The arm. Who was that? Where's the person that was waving me in?*

"Hello?" Only the sound of a muffled echo reverberated back at me from all directions. "Hello?"

Nothing.

A slight melodic humming noise filled the air.

"Hello?" I coughed and grimaced in pain as I tried to get to my feet. The slight humming noise seemed to respond to me. Whatever that stench was, it was now getting to me.

I felt chills over my body again. I was starting to panic. For all I knew, the person that waved me in there could be right in front of my face, but it was too dark to see.

"Where are you? I saw someone wave at me!" My voice was gaining volume as I started losing my patience. The hum again sounded like some sort of musical instrument, but it was a chilling sound. "Hello? I saw you! Where'd you go?"

I was about to yell again when something soft brushed against my face. It felt like the feathers inside a pillow. Wiping at my mouth and reaching my arms out, I staggered backward in haste. The darkness was much too thick and I couldn't see anything around me.

Suddenly, I heard what sounded like whispers in the distance. The whispers and the humming seemed to mimic each other.

"Are you there? Where are you?" Silence. "Hello?" I asked.

I held out my arms again to search the area in front of me, but I couldn't feel anything. I was hesitant at first, but after feeling nothing, I began waving my arms around like a mad man. My ribs were on fire. I coughed again and groaned deeply.

As I coughed a third time, there was another brush against my face, still soft but with more pressure. The whispers got louder for a brief moment, but I couldn't understand anything they were saying.

"Come on!" I shouted. "I know you're here! Show yourself! What's happening? I need medical attention!"

Now, an even more forceful brush came to my face. It startled me so much that I fell backward to the hard floor of the cave. I groaned audibly again.

I slowly stood up again. I started waving my hands in front of my face wildly.

Then it happened. I saw it.

Light.

It was a gradual illumination from a tiny ball-sized flame to a lamp. I had never seen a light fade up like that before in such a condensed space. It was like a sunrise was captured and confined to a small area just in front of me. It wasn't orange like a sunrise though, at times it was more of a yellow or green color. I felt my eyes widen as I took a step back.

A silhouette of a person wearing a robe-like covering slowly appeared as if it stepped out of the light. There was a bright, white light where it's face should've been. I couldn't make out anything about the figure. I still had no idea where the light was coming from, but it was brightening the area around me. I could make out a cobblestone floor and large, smooth stone for walls.

The figure was extremely small. I would've guessed a child. The light emanating from behind it was really strange.

"Wh… what are you? Who… are you?" I managed to stammer out. "I'm..." I couldn't even remember my spec number. Silently, I moved back as it lifted its arm and reached out to touch me.

I felt my skin tingle and my body surge with energy as it touched me. It was a strange, but lovely sensation. I had never felt anything like it ever before. I didn't want to move from it, but as suddenly as the sensation came, it was gone.

The light grew, but I still couldn't make out anything other than its form. I noticed as the light grew and saturated the area around me, the stench decreased and the whispers were silenced. I could smell the earth around me again. I could smell the moss and mud that I previously rubbed all over me. I even thought I smelled the scent of fresh apples.

It was almost as if the light acted as some kind of bubble around me. My body felt strange. I didn't know if I felt the pain anymore. For one moment, I had forgotten what the pain of my broken body was supposed to feel like.

"You must be silent." It finally spoke, as three distinct voices together as one. It was haunting and calming all at the same time. "It will hear you, and when it hears you, it will overtake you."

I'm dreaming this, surely I am. I'm unconscious. I'm dead.

"What will hear me? Who?" I asked.

"You must be silent. It'll find." The voice was singular now. "But when you're ready, *you* will overcome *him*."

"When I'm ready? Ready for what? What are you talking about? Can you take me somewhere to get help? I can't go to the hospital, they'll know I'm a specimen." I held my ribs. As I touched them, they started throbbing again. They were pulsating with sharp pinches when I inhaled and exhaled.

"Stop," the voice said as it touched me again. The feeling returned to me and sent a jolt of ecstasy through me.

"Wha…" I couldn't even speak. I didn't know what it was, but I wanted more of it.

"I called you out." All three voices said again. "You're here because you have been chosen."

"Chosen? No, I'm here because I escaped, and as I was running from the guards, I saw someone motion me in here, which I'm assuming was you." I grimaced as it stopped touching me.

"You were drawn here." The light was growing dim. "You have been chosen, but you must surrender or it will get you too."

Surrender? To X? Why would I want to do that?

"Me too? Have there been others? Are there others now? Surrender to what?" I asked. *This is just a trip,* I tried to convince myself. It was common for spec testing to cause crazy hallucinations often.

"Know me and you will see the truth." By now the arm pointing toward the direction from which I had fallen. "Love is the greatest form of energy. Become hope. Set them free."

"Hope? Isn't hope just a beggar? I..." *This is crazy.* I turned to look to see if I could make out the stairs from behind me. I couldn't. I winced as the light was quickly fading.

When I turned again, the light was gone. The smell had returned, but it was much worse. The whispers seemed to be all around me. They almost sounded as if they were children. I couldn't understand what they were saying. It sounded as if it was a different language.

"Hello?" I spoke into the air again. The melodic humming noise returned. How I could be in this much pain and dreaming is completely insane to me. *Am I hallucinating from the pain?*

I must wake up! I slapped myself in the face, but when I did I hit my ear that had been cut during the fall.

I cursed. I screamed. I shouted, "wake up! Wake up, you fool!"

In total pain and agony, I screamed again. The ground began shaking. The stone walls were vibrating. Dirt from above me fell to my head. I looked up to see the outline of roots draping like stalactites in a cave. A dim reddish-orange light was flickering in front of me and I could begin to make out a tunnel. The light appeared like a fire that was spreading. It was headed toward me. The louder I screamed, the more illuminated the area became.

I started crying like a complete fool. Louder and more violently, I heard the sound of my own voice climbing. I was frustrated that I couldn't wake myself up. The more I panicked, the more severe the walls and ground shook.

The light was so bright now that I could see all around me. However, I couldn't see the figure that was talking to me just a moment ago.

I started dry-heaving again. I was terrified.

My feet were lifted from the ground as the orange color grew brighter and came closer. My arms felt like they were being ripped from their sockets. I was certain that my ribs were being pulled from underneath my flesh. I screamed.

My body was violently spun upside down so I could make out the ceiling of the cave. I could recognize the outline of bodies everywhere above me in translucent sarcophaguses. Roots perturbed from the ceiling from the trees above the ground. They started to move around like they were snakes, trying to grab at me.

I started to panic. *Why can't I wake up? I've never had a nightmare like this before.*

In fear, I screamed. In pain, I cried. In desperation, I yelled for whoever could hear me. I knew that my heart was just moments away from bursting.

Being propelled by some unseen force into the stalactite-like roots and bodies, I started to claw my way back toward the direction from which I entered the cave. Dreaming or not, I wanted out. I was determined to not let myself end up like one of those bodies in their cocoons.

I came face to face with one of the bodies. The sarcophagi smelled terrible. I assumed they were dead, until I was startled by one of them beginning to yell, "Help us! Get us out of here!"

Each body, in their smoky covering, started to awaken and try to break free.

"Get me out of here!" They screamed in a haunting chorus.

Grabbing tree roots and clumps of the ceiling, I clawed my way back as fast as I could. Something in my head was warning me about the approaching light. I knew that I had to avoid it.

With every movement I made, my ribs burned with intense pain. My head pounded. The more I resisted the invisible force, the more it felt like a thousand pounds of pressure hammering against my skull.

The light was all around me. The smell was so unbearable, it burned my nostrils.

"Become hope! Set them free!" I heard the other three voices chanting. There was such a contrast between the two entities.

Clawing my way closer and closer toward the opening, I could finally make out the light from the sun now breaking through the roots of the tree. *Almost there*, I told myself. The roots of the trees became like snakes trying to wrap themselves around my body as I struggled to get out of the cave.

If I did make it out, I was certain that X would be there waiting for me with the dogs ready to rip me limb from limb? What would be worse: becoming shredded beef by some angry militant mutts, or becoming prey to whatever this thing was?

A loud, violent sound filled my ears and the cave beneath me as I continued to reach and claw toward my exit. I thought it resembled a horn or a siren, or maybe a scream. Whatever it was, the sound made me physically ill.

The roots continued to reach for me and try to pull me in. One more push was all I needed to break free, but my body was in so much pain that I didn't think I had anything left. The more I fought, the more I struggled against whatever this was.

Unaware of what was around me, as my body was completely parallel to the ceiling of the cave, I reached my arm out as far as I could. My body was becoming sucked into the roof of the cavern. "Help me! Help me!" I shouted. I started to taste dirt in my mouth. I spat it out, but I could feel myself breathing in tiny granules. I felt my hand emerge from the ground as if the earth was opening to give birth to me. I didn't have the energy to wrap my mind around what was happening. I felt a voice in my head telling me to surrender.

Surrender? I can't possible surrender. I need to fight!

Then suddenly, I felt the warmth of a human hand reaching for mine from beyond the opening. The hand held on tightly and I felt it pull. I then felt a second hand pulling me through the ground.

Between the hands from the outside pulling at me and the force pulling me into the cave, I felt like I was being ripped in half.

"Surrender," a still, small voice whispered in my head.

I fought and pushed against the force, but I was running out of energy. I started screaming as I tried to use all the strength I had left to push my way out.

Help me. Help! Please. I'll do whatever. Just help me!

"Surrender," the voice repeated itself.

"I can't!" I yelled. "Help me!"

My abdomen felt like it started to tear apart as I was being pulled in two directions. "Help!" I screamed as I tried to fight. I felt my head begin to go faint like I was going to pass out. I didn't know what to do. *Maybe I should give up, or surrender. What's the difference anyway?*

I sighed and breathed in a deep breath as I screamed, "Fine! I surrender!"

My entire body went limp as I was extracted through the opening.

Being moved into the fresh air now, my maliciously mangled body lay crumpled on the soft forest floor. I could feel the warm and wondrous sensation of sunlight on my skin again. The stench of sulfur was gone and I thought at the time, I could even smell the needles from the red pine trees.

Officer X128 stood over my broken body. How was it that the person I hated the most had just become my savior? He looked at me, perplexed. "229, get a gurney down here immediately!"

Officer X229 motioned to a couple of medic officers who were already making their way down, jumping over limbs and rocks.

What was this? Compassion? X stood over me, but instead of the satisfied look of doing his job and catching the escapee, his face was in shock. He looked at me, then the tree roots, and then again at me. He reached for the roots to see if he could find an opening, he clawed at the tree and surrounding dirt. I watched as he frantically looked for an explanation.

I was one step away from finally passing out, but I listened in to what the medics said as they reached my damaged body.

"This is new." 229 said. "We've never had one return. Did you see where he went in?"

X shook his head and was without words, for once in his life. “No,” he mumbled. He stood and directed the medics toward me. They loaded me carefully onto the gurney and hauled me back toward the road.

“Find me in the stillness. Find me in the silence.” I heard the voices like whispers in the air around me. At the same time, I watched a group of birds overhead fly from the tree they were perched upon. I tired to look at the men, but they didn’t seemed to be fazed by the whispers. *Did they not hear that?*

I felt the medics begin to carry me on the stretcher and walk slowly through the forest.

“Spec, can you hear me?” One of the medics was trying to talk to me in a whisper as they carried me out. “If you can hear me, blink.”

I blinked.

The same medic looked to be on the verge of tears. I could recognize him. *Mark.* He was one of the same medics that were always assigned to spec detail. He often assisted in the dorm if a test got out of hand.

“Did you see him?” He asked in a whisper, being very obvious that he didn’t want the others to hear him. “Is it true? Does it exist?”

I laid there, unable to speak.

“Excuse me, Mark.” X turned with his taser drawn. The medic dropped his end of the gurney. My head bounced off the ground as the gurney fell. “Are you talking to the patient when you know that this is against protocol?”

X shot the man with his taser. The medic fell back out of my sight. A quick and chilling sound of X breaking the man’s neck now filled my ears. A shot of fear pierced me, but I had no power left to run. I exhausted myself with even the thought of running.

I whimpered and coughed as I felt tears fill my eyes.

Officer X229 stepped into my view. "Come on, X! Was that really necessary?"

"What are you talking about, officer?" He looked at all of the surrounding men. "This medic died from a fatal injury during a training exercise today. Copperline has suffered a great loss today." X looked to everyone standing around him as they all nodded without seeming to have any emotion at all. "Let's hurry and get this trash to containment."

Then it hit me. I felt the butt end of X's taser against my temple.

Out.

Two

"What are you talking about?" Mayor Martin Black stared Officer X128 in the eyes and kept his voice low so other people wouldn't hear them talk. "A spec. A spec killed a medic? *That* spec killed *that* medic?"

"That is correct, sir," X128 responded with no emotion.

"Stick with the story that Mark died in a training exercise. Understood?" He asked the officer.

X128 nodded.

"Did the spec make into the tree?" Mayor Black lowered his voice even more.

X128 surveyed to see if people were noticing the two of them talking. "Not only did it make it in, but it came back out. It was screaming and its body was shaking. I thought it was going to die, but it survived. It's in a coma now."

Mayor Black turned and leaned against a wall. He clenched his jaw and closed his eyes. "That's never happened before, right?"

"Correct. It was almost like it preferred to be in our custody over whatever was going on inside, or underneath the tree." X crossed his arms once the Mayor leaned against the wall.

"Why didn't you find a way in?" The mayor asked. "It's got to be the portal," he mumbled to himself.

"I tried, but it just looked like a big red pine tree that fell over. There didn't seem to be anything special about *this* tree." X's eyes still nervously watched the people around them in the courtyard.

"Wait, when did the spec attack the medic?" Mayor Black got in X's face again. "Your story is becoming harder to believe. Quite honestly, I don't care about the medic, but your story has to line up. You can lie to them, but don't you ever lie to me." He drove his finger into X's chest.

"Sir…" X hung his head. "It just got out of hand, fast. I didn't know what to do or think. A lot of strange events… I can't explain. I recommend we hire an outside contractor to remove the tree." X knew that Mayor Black would be momentarily distracted by the request.

"We can't do that. It would cause too much suspicion," the mayor said, annoyed by X's suggestion.

X nodded. "What is it about that tree? Why are all the specs running there? Could the specs become an issue to the city?"

"Don't be stupid and don't change the subject! The citizens don't even know the specs exist. You may have just opened a door to something unpleasant." Mayor Black backed off from X when he noticed his secretary entering the opposite end of the courtyard. "I can count on you, Gerald," the mayor said just above a whisper. "I can count on you, right?"

Martin was trying not to make assumptions until he had a chance to meet with the spec himself. Covering up an unfortunate death of one of the citizens was not a hard task for the mayor and his team. This would be nothing more than a little wrinkle in the fabric of superiority.

He fixed his tie and straightened his jacket. "Please make sure our medic has the most appropriate celebration of life!" The Mayor said in a chipper tone when he noticed his secretary approaching the two men. He leaned into X once more and whispered, "this isn't over."

X nodded and took the door leading to the conference room, where he would give his account of what happened today. The guard would go live on Copperline Television to give a statement of his version of the truth.

Martin's secretary approached the Mayor. Her darker skin contrasted his, but he was always attracted to her dark eyes. He always preferred her perfume over his wife's. He returned her smile. "Maria, can you please clear my schedule for the rest of the day? I need to gather my thoughts and get ready for the Celebration of Life for Mark."

Maria smiled and put a hand on Martin's shoulder. "Of course, Mayor."

As Maria walked away, Martin turned from her and headed in the direction of his office. His smile quickly turned to a frown as he hastily left the courtyard.

Martin took pride in his city. Copperline was regarded as the most efficient and desirable place to live in the eyes of Americans. It had been featured on several TV shows, magazines, newspaper articles, and Hollywood even referenced it in a movie one time. For people everywhere, it was viewed as a utopia of sorts. From its manicured streets and perfect lawns to its promise of safety and incredible education, it was a little slice of perfection. The top medical researches lived in the city and worked with a team of practitioners known for their success.

Originally created to be a retirement community, James Hurd and his team of contractors, politicians, doctors, and teachers, crafted a safe haven for all who resided in it. However, Martin Black's purpose was to create excellence in humanity that was lacking in the rest of the country.

He wanted a place that made the rich feel pampered, and gave advancement for the young. The residents ranged from retired business people who put a lot of their wealth back into the city to younger families desiring to get great education. Young, extraordinary minds of student candidates would eventually become part of the city's expansion plan for the future.

Martin was one of the only town officials to have complete contact with any of the outside world. He had full access to the internet as well as every news station. This was a decision that was made between the city council early in the '90s when the internet started booming. It was perceived by city officials to be potentially harmful, so it was never introduced to the older citizens. The internet was not accessible or desirable for the people of Copperline, neither was cable television. Most people in Copperline didn't need anything more than a landline telephone and the CTV network.

The local government secretly monitored every phone call and read every piece of mail before it was delivered to citizens. Residential and commercial structures were equipped with closed-circuit cameras. With approximately 100,000 tiny cameras throughout the city, the surveillance teams had a close eye on the people. With security guards watching random feeds at all times, it was unlikely that anything was kept from the council.

Copperline's walls were protected by unseen electrically-charged lines that followed the shape of designs within the brick facade. However, from inside the city, residents saw a beautiful tree line that separated the city and the wall.

Visitors were limited and approved by only the city council prior to each visit. It was impossible for even an unannounced state official to breach the walls of the gated city.

"The perfect system." Mayor Black said to himself as he looked out the window of his office overlooking the courtyard.

"She's the système parfait, and we can't have one disobedient spec ruining that for us."

Martin walked over to the phone on his desk and dialed the extension to the hospital.

"Copperline General, how may I direct your call?"

"Jenny, this is Mayor Black. How are you doing today?" Martin asked in a soft tone.

"Oh, Mayor Black! I'm fine, thank you! And you?"

"I'm saddened with the loss of one of our fine medics, but it's important that we celebrate a life that served this city diligently for many years." Martin kept his tone appropriately sympathetic.

"Yes, it is so tragic. We celebrate and mourn. Can I direct your call to the morgue?"

"No, Jenny. I need to speak to Doctor Jacobs in the lab, please."

"Yes, sir. Please hold. It was lovely talking to you today," Jenny said before the line transferred to the lab.

"Jacobs." A scruffy voice abruptly interrupted the short stillness.

"David, it's Martin. What are we looking at here?" The sympathetic tone was gone in Martin's voice. David was a number of years older than Martin, but they worked together with the alchemists ever since the Mayor took office.

"Martin, I don't even know what to make of this. He's been…"

"David, Stop! I told you to never refer to the specs as he or she. They are specimens. Don't make this personal by giving it a gender." Martin's raised his voice at the doctor.

"Martin, relax. I'm not making any of this personal, but we have something that I've never seen in a number of years. We put it in a medically induced coma since we received it from the guards. It's broken several bones and *had* a lot of internal bleeding." Martin heard David flipping through papers. "But there's more."

"What do you mean it *had* internal bleeding? It hasn't been there long enough for surgery." Martin looked at his watch, already aggravated that the conversation had gone longer than he wanted.

"It seems to be healing itself rather quickly. More quickly than I've ever seen a body heal." Martin could sense the nervous tone in David's voice. "It also seems to be raising its pH balance and body heat, but it doesn't seem like a fever. It's somehow also emitting questionable levels of radiation. I've only seen that once in…"

"No fever?" Martin immediately interrupted him. He winced as he looked out his office window.

"The pH balance in his body is extremely high," David began explaining. "A lot like yours, but quite higher. I'm not sure as to why he would be this way. I know the diet in the spec dorm wouldn't contribute to a high pH balance. I don't know…"

"Don't know? David, you are the most brilliant minds I'm acquainted with. 'Don't know' is not good enough." Martin could feel himself losing his patience. He sat at his desk with a hand on his forehead and one hand holding the receiver. *Calm down, you fool. A spec is not worth it.* "Look, David. My officer gave me more information."

"What? Any new information will be great."

"X128 said that he pulled it out of the tree." Martin paused

"The *same* tree? Is this the first time one made it out?"

"Yes. X128 said how it was screaming for help like it wanted to come out. No other spec has ever escaped. The officer even tried to find an opening or portal, but he couldn't find anything." Martin's voice was softer now.

"What happened inside that tree?" David mumbled. "Once it's awake, I'll give it the truth serum and see what he says."

"Hold off until I get there. For now, just try threatening with the serum first to see if it talks."

Martin was momentarily distracted as his wife's extension come up on his desk phone. "David, Sarah is calling. Meet me in the courtyard tonight at four. Let's talk again."

Martin switched lines on his phone. "Sarah? You know never to call me here."

The line was filled with static and the muffled sound of crying. "Martin?"

"Sarah? Sarah, what is it?" Martin said uneasily. "Answer me, please."

"Martin!"

Three

"He's waking up." I heard a female voice say. I opened my eyes slowly to adjust to the harsh fluorescent light. A nurse was approaching me as I laid still. "Spec? Can you hear me?"

I nodded.

I noticed my neck and ribs didn't hurt anymore. *How long was I out? Where am I?*

The nurse was a seemingly pleasant woman. I figured she had to be almost retirement age with her silver hair. In the spec dorms, we never had pleasant nurses or doctors. Each person that we experienced looked at us like we were trash, but she had a simple and lovely smile on her face.

I tried to move my hand to feel my ear, but I saw that I was strapped to the bed. I felt nylon straps around my wrists as I tried to pull against my restraints. *No pain?*

"Why…" I tried to talk, but my throat was dry and raspy.

"Hold on, dear. Let me adjust the bed and give you some water." The nurse moved toward the bed and pushed a button on a remote. My bed moved to more of an upright position.

She called me dear. I instantly felt like this woman legitimately cared.

While reaching for water, she started humming a tune. A familiar tune, but I couldn't quite place it. *What is that tune?* I've always heard about sounds or smells that bring you back to certain times, but I had no recollection of what this tune could be from. It made me feel sad, happy, pain, joy, and confusion all at the same time. *What was this, and why is it making me feel so many emotions?* It was like that song cast a spell on me.

"Ma'am, what are you…" Still my throat.

"Don't strain your voice." The nurse put the glass to my lips.

As I drank the water, my eyes searched the room. I was noticing that my senses seemed intensified. Hearing, smelling, sight, and even my taste. I noticed small details that I never thought to give attention to before. I noticed the almost invisible triangular detection lines in the window. I've always known they were there, but I could never see them. I've heard stories of specs trying to break through, only to get a deadly shock. I've always wondered how much electricity actually shot through those lines. I wondered if I could withstand the jolt.

I was hearing the second hand on the clock as if someone was tapping a hammer against the wall.

I could feel my muscles in my arms as I flexed them slightly against the restraints. I wondered if I could break them.

The nurse put the cup down and smiled at me again. I heard the gentle ting of the glass as she placed it on a metal table.

There was a distinct smell in the air. *A familiar smell. What is that? I think that's the smell of blood.*

The nurse was still humming the tune as she continued to cleaned up the room. I wanted to ask her name, or ask what they gave me to make me feel so alive. I never remembering ever feeling like this. I felt rested and energetic.

I looked at the window again and wondered if I could break out.

Even if *I* was to shatter the glass and withstand the electricity, I'm not sure I could survive the fall. I must've been five floors up in the Containment Lab. I remembered rumors from other specs who described this very room. I'd been in something like this before, but that was usually a solid concrete-walled room with no window.

However, this room was different than what I was used to. This bed was more desirable than the mattress that I had in my dorm room. My resting place was nothing more than a few pads of styrofoam with a sheet. This in contrast was really nice. It felt like I was laying down on cushion. I wondered if this was what kind of mattresses all the residence had.

"What are you humming?" I finally asked.

She smiled. "It's an old lullaby that I knew from before I lived and worked in Copperline. I can't remember the name, but I used to sing it to my children." The nurse paused for a minute and smiled again as she looked me right in the eyes.

She looked in my eyes. I wasn't used to this kind of treatment from a medical professional. They would usually never look us in the eyes, especially when they were torturing us.

"Do you have children in Copperline?" I had to know more about the tune that somehow had so much power over me.

"Yes. Two daughters, and now they each have two children of their own, here in the city." She smiled once more as she resumed tidying up the room.

That's when I noticed a lot of needles and saline bags. I looked at bloody cloths strewed all over the floor around my bed. *Mine?* There was blood on the floor. *Wait? Did I really fall down that stone staircase under that tree? It wasn't a dream?*

I tried to remember what happened to me without convincing myself I was a complete psychopath? I looked more around the room to see if I could notice anything else significant. I wanted to ask about the blood on the floor. I had to know if it was mine. I wanted to know what all the syringes and saline bags were used for.

"How long have I been out?" I asked.

"Just a few hours." She lowered her voice. "You started to regain consciousness when you were initially brought to us, but then there was a struggle, so they had to put you out." She said as she continued to clean the room. "You healed at a remarkable and unexplainable…"

"That's enough, Nurse." A doctor entered the room with a scowl on his face and his hands behind his back. He started walking slowly over to me. The large glass door slid shut behind him. "You are simply supposed to be cleaning, and not interacting with the spec."

Her countenance completely changed. "I'm sorry, Dr. I just thought…"

"You thought? I'm terribly sorry, my dear. Don't think. Thinking in this instance could make for unfortunate circumstances that you would regret. We wouldn't want that, right?" Dr. David Jacobs grabbed the nurse's chin and forced her to look at him. "We've already had one unfortunate accident today. I'd certainly hate to hear about another." He let go of her chin and smiled. "Now get back to work, please."

"Sir." The nurse said as she turned her face away.

She continued to clean the room, but without a smile and absolutely no humming. In one moment, this man had completely taken the oxygen from the room. He approached me, examining a couple different monitors just above my bed.

I read his name tag. "Dr. David Jacobs, MD. Residency: DTS."

DTS? Downtown Sector? I asked myself.

I've heard a spec or two talk about a Dr. Jacobs. I heard that he works with the alchemists and creates the vaccines and serums they test on us, specs. We're treated like animal testing subjects as to perfect the formulas. They wait to see what side effects we contract before they administer it to the residents. I guess the citizens are only the second round of testing before they sell the drugs to pharmaceuticals throughout the country. *I hate this guy already.*

"One thing I want to know," he said to me, but didn't bother to look. "What happened in that tree?"

"The tree?" I knew if I didn't give him what he wanted, he'd pull out a syringe with truth serum and I hated that stuff. I hated the way it made me feel after. Sometimes I'd even have a headache for days after a dose. "I remember falling in a sinkhole. That's where I got my injuries."

"You and I know it was more than that, wasn't it?" he asked. "I'd hate to…"

"Fill my veins full of truth?" I knew where he was heading with this. I clenched my firsts. I felt the nylon straps get tighter. I felt like I could've broken the straps.

"Don't interrupt me, spec. You *should* be dead. You murdered one of our medics earlier today and you will eventually be put on trial." He snapped his head toward me but still wouldn't look at me.

I didn't murder anybody, did I? No! That was X. He murdered Mark. What is happening here? I asked myself as I tried to remember.

"Now tell me. What happened in that tree?" He whispered.

The room went quiet for an awkward amount of time. The only sounds were from the old woman who had dropped something on the floor. "Nurse! Leave the room."

"Sir." The nurse nodded as she left.

"I didn't kill any…" I tried to say, but my throat went dry again. I coughed. "I didn't kill anyone!"

He stood silent.

I knew I had to give him something, but something inside, something was warning me not to tell him everything I experienced. Although, I'm not even really sure for myself exactly what I experienced. "I fell down and was pinned under the tree somehow. X…"

"X?" He asked.

"Officer X128 pulled me from underneath the tree." I looked to see if this appeased him. I couldn't tell. He stood there silent with his hands behind his back.

"There's more that you're not telling me." He wasn't appeased. "I know that there is something inside, or under, or around that tree. Something happened to you. You changed. I see from your chart, your last physical exam was only two weeks ago. Your pH balance, your resting heart rate, your eyes." He paused for a second. "Yes, your eyes have changed. Changes like these don't just occur magically, Spec. What happened?"

"I'm telling you." I looked down as I spoke. "I fell in a sink hole and I thought it would be safer in the facility where I belonged."

"What makes you think you belong anywhere?" This time Jacobs' eyes were glaring right into mine. His voice also changed to a dark and deep tone.

He looked back at the monitor with his hands behind his back. His clean, white lab coat was without wrinkle or any imperfection.

"It is quite incredible though." He cleared throat. "You have no more fractures. No more bruising. The wounds have completely healed. Your ear has even seemed to… grow back?" He tapped the screen again, then turned toward me. "Why?"

I wondered the same thing. *Why? What really happened? The nurse said there was a struggle, and the room was showing evidence of a mess. Was that my blood on the floor? I know I didn't kill Mark. I really liked Mark, but did I actually kill someone in transition?* I remembered Jacobs said that there was one death as he threatened the nurse. *They're trying to frame me for Mark's death.*

"Why are you healing so quickly?"

"I already told you everything I know." I tried to come up with something to say.

"You have told me nothing!" He yelled. He looked directly at me again, but this time he took one hand from behind his back and grabbed my chin. Softening his voice, he looked at my eyes. "And your eyes. Why have they changed?"

I had no idea what my eyes normally looked like, but I know all my fellow specs have the same bloodshot eyes as a result of all the testing and torture. *Why does he keep mentioning my eyes?* In the spec dorms, we're not allowed mirrors. I have never seen a clear reflection of myself. The closest I got to a reflection was the back of a stainless steel cereal bowl that I used as a mirror to shave every other day.

"I'll give you one more chance to hit me with the truth before I hit you with it," he said.

I cringed at the terrible cliche. My hatred for the man grew incredibly.

Looking down, I really tried to formulate something believable. I couldn't go with the 'tiny spirit -guy living in the cave under the tree who told me to set the people free' story.

"I told you." I looked up at him and shook my head. *I had nothing.* I sighed.

"You fell under the tree somehow." He said sarcastically. Shaking his head to mimic mine. He took another step closer to me. Finally, his right arm that was once held behind his back all this time, swung out toward me. I could see it. The syringe.

No! Not today!

Before I realized I had even done it. My left hand snapped the nylon strap and I grabbed his arm out of defense. I could feel his cold skin.

He looked at me in confusion and terror and dropped the syringe. It bounced off the side of the bed, then hit the floor.

My grip was tight on his arm. For a brief moment, we were both frozen disbelief. Then he started trying to pull his arm back, but I let it go. I didn't actually want to hurt him and I didn't want him to fill my bloodstream full of that poison.

He quickly dove for the syringe while I tried to break my other arm free, but I couldn't. *Come on, spec. Don't overthink it, just do it.* Instead, every time I tried to break my arm free from the strap, my head pounded with such pain. It was like a terrible migraine or like a flood of blood rushing into my head and punishing me with such extraordinary pain.

With each tug of my arm, the pressure increased in my head to the point where the room was spinning. I couldn't help it. I started screaming.

Jacobs grabbed the syringe, but as he came to his feet and saw me, he stood still in disbelief. "How is this possible?" he whispered. He appeared to be in great fear.

Screaming and trying to pull my arm out of the nylon strap, I noticed him move away from me. His face was riddled in confusion. He started shaking his head.

What does he see? What is happening to me?

The pain in my head pulsated. The room was a whirlwind around me as I screamed. I could see the lights flickering above me. I became so dizzy, I had the sudden urge to throw up.

Jacobs moved back and pinned himself to the wall by the intercom. He put the syringe in one of his lab coat pockets and hit the talk button on the wall.

"This is Dr. Jacobs! The patient is doing it again! Get Mayor Black down here now!" His shouts were loud and filled with terror.

Jacobs moved his hand from the talk button to a panic alarm. A sliding door opened and a number of male nurses ran into the room with medical equipment. Suddenly the room was filled with the horrible, ear-piercing alarm that filled my head with more pressure.

"Shut it off! Stop this! What is happening to me?" I shouted as my body began to shake uncontrollably. "What are you doing to me?" I watched as my veins turned dark blue under my flesh.

I felt warm tears stream from my eyes to my chin. My heart rate was increasing. My sight was going dim. I could see that I was vomiting red fluid. *Blood? Was that the blood all over the floor?*

My breathing was becoming labored and shallow, but I could still hear the sound of people rushing into the room. They were yelling at each other and ordering each other around with medical terms that I couldn't understand.

Then in an instant.

Darkness.

Stillness.

Silence.

My body stopped shaking. No more pressure in my head. No eyesight. I could no longer hear the sounds of the people rushing around me. No piercing alarm sound.

Just stillness.

Suddenly, I was watching my body as if I stood over it, but the room was completely black. I couldn't see nurses or doctors. The only thing illuminated was my hospital bed. I couldn't see my face either. I wanted desperately to see what my eyes looked like.

I wondered if I was dead. I asked myself if I should I expect to slip into the afterlife and come face to face with some kind of divine maker? *Were the fables true?* I've read stories from an ancient book that taught of a maker. Elohim, I think his name was. *Am I about to meet Elohim?*

I noticed I didn't have the sensation of breathing. I couldn't feel my tongue lying against my bottom teeth. I couldn't feel the mattress underneath my body.

I feel nothing but pure emptiness.

"Daniel," a soft chorus of whispers came from inside my head. "Rest, Daniel. Don't hurt them."

Daniel? Was that my name?

I tried to speak, but I couldn't. I didn't know how to make even the smallest utterance in this state.

I was overwhelmed emotionally. I thought that if I could physically do so, I would cry out.

Elohim? I thought. I tried to remember every book I had ever read that Mark smuggled in. *Was there something like this? Anything that would help me? Was this what was known in the books as magic? This isn't magic, it?*

But in a split-second, the sight of the hospital bed was instantly taken from me with the sound of a loud rush of wind.

The faint sound of the alarm returned to my ears, but my head wasn't pounding anymore. I could feel the ground underneath my feet. *Am I standing?* I could smell the room again. *Was something burning?* It smelled like a combination of an electrical fire and burning flesh.

I felt my lungs breathing again. I could feel my heart beating and the dryness in my mouth as I inhaled. I felt the urge to open my eyes. Slowly opening my eyelids, they quickly adjusted to a dimly lit containment room.

I looked upon complete destruction. I stared in disbelief at chaos. Bodies were lying everywhere around me. One of the male nurses was still holding the paddles to what looked like a defibrillator, but his hands were burned to a crisp. Another nurse looked as if gunpowder blew up in his face.

I noticed they were all still breathing. One female nurse was in the corner hiding under a metal table whimpering while holding her ankles looking in an opposite direction. I immediately felt pity on her.

What happened?

Where is Jacobs?

I surveyed the room. The thick glass was cracked, but still inside the frame. Light fixtures were flickering on and off while they hung from the ceiling. It looked as if it were out of a scene of a fictional war book and the lab had just taken a hit from a bomb.

Jacobs wasn't in the room. *Where did he go? How do I get out?*

I began moving slowly to the nurses to see if I could get answers. Whatever happened while I was unconscious, I'm sure I didn't mean to do any of this. *Did I do this though? How could I?*

Stepping over tables and other items that I had no idea as to what they were, I bent down to try to take the defibrillator paddles from the man's hands. As I touched his finger to try to pull it away from the paddle, I realized they were grafted to the paddle. I pulled my hand back quickly in disgust.

The sensation of pain must've come back to him. He snapped his eyes open and began to yell. His mouth gaping wide in a pain-induced scream.

"My hands! My hands! I can't- I can't let go. It's burning!" He made eye contact with me. Tears instantly filled his eyes. His face was in shock. His mouth was agape. "Y- You… What? How?" He looked again to his paddles, then again to me. In shock and disbelief, it was clear to me this man was terrified of me now.

"Sir, what happened?" I asked in a quiet voice. "I'm so sorry, I don't know what I did."

"We tried to shock you when your heart stopped, and… I have never… I don't even know…" He stammered through his words. "It backfired! The machine blew up!" He groaned in agony as he continued to look at his hands.

"Not another word, nurse!" A voice from the intercom shouted. I lifted my head to see Jacobs standing on the other side of the cracked glass. He looked a lot more confident *behind* the glass door. He didn't have the same fear-stricken face that he did just a moment ago.

Am I becoming a monster? I never meant to hurt anybody. Did I cause this?

I looked to the nurse on the floor again still moaning in pain trying to pull his hands away from the paddle. He looked up at me again, but then I saw that his sight was diverted to something behind me.

Then I remembered, the other nurse that was in the corner. I noticed a slight reflection in the glass from the sliding door. She had lifted a syringe up and quickly drove it into my back as I felt my body become limp and drop to the solid, cold floor.

Out. Again.

Four

Martin approached the large white Victorian mansion from the end of his long driveway. He brought his cart to a stop and quickly walked to the porch of his estate. Trying not to make it look obvious that something was wrong, he developed the practice of keeping his composure at all times. He passed several citizens from the citadel to his manor. He would commonly and politely wave while reciting the usual “Hello, neighbor!”

Martin knew that people would cue their thoughts and feelings off his countenance, so he always tried to remain confidently composed even amidst absolute chaos. Though he had no idea what he was walking into at his home, the residents didn’t need to know that Sarah Black had called her husband in a panic.

Entering the house, a pungent and familiar smell hit him so that he lifted his forearm to shelter his nose.

“Sarah?” He started to walk from the foyer into the great room. “Sarah?”

Bradley, Martin’s 10-year-old son came around the corner and met him with a cloth over his nose and mouth. Martin recognized the print from one of his wife’s kitchen cloths.

"Bradley, what is that smell? Where is your mother?" Martin said to the boy. Bradley stood there with a blue button shirt tucked into khaki pants.

"She's in the kitchen. The stove exploded, father!" Bradley said while extending his arms wide.

"Son, don't talk with your hands. It's obnoxious. Why don't you open some of these windows and let the house air out," Martin said lifting his gaze from his son to the kitchen.

"Margret and I tried, but they wouldn't open." Bradley pointed to the great room windows. Each latch had been opened, and Martin could see that they had attempted to open them.

The scent that hung in the air gave the Mayor a certain sense of uneasiness. *Why now?*

Martin, still holding his forearm to his nose, made his way over to a window and moved the latch around and tried to open it. The window seemed to have shifted in its frame. "Did the explosion… The stove explosion did this?" He tried the window next to it, this time using both of his hands to prop it open. The window finally budged and he managed to open it a crack.

"There. See that, son? Just open the rest of them like that."

Bradley nodded and jumped on the opportunity to make his father proud.

Martin made his way to the kitchen, catching his feet on hardwood floorboards that were popping up. *What is that from?*

Grabbing one of Margret's scarfs from the sofa, he tied it around his head to mask his nose from the sulfuric smell. He knew that he must've looked ridiculous, and he would never allow the citizens to see him in a moment of weakness.

"Sarah?" He called out and peered slowly around the opening to the kitchen, not knowing what to expect.

He noticed more flooring underneath his feet that were obviously out of place.

"Looks like I should get Henry in to redo our flooring. It's probably about time anyway." He said as he made his way into the kitchen to see his wife inspecting the oven.

Sarah was practically inside the oven, putting the oven grates back in their place.

"Martin, I'm sorry I pulled you from your office. I know I overreacted," she said.

"Overreacting only creates problems that don't yet exist," Martin replied shaking his head.

"The propane must've been running. I set the oven to preheat so I could make dinner for Mellissa and give it to her tonight at Mark's celebration of life, and it just blew." She gestured her hands as she explained the situation.

"Sarah, please don't talk with your hands," the Mayor said as he rolled his eyes.

"Margret is upstairs scared," Sarah continued to say as if her husband had never interrupted her. She stood there with her hands on her hips.

Margret is always scared, he thought. He didn't understand what was going on with that daughter of his. She was very finicky as of late.

"Sarah." Martin put a hand on her shoulder. He pulled her close to him. She fell into him and put her arms around his back. "You need to pull it together."

Sarah backed off from him and studied his face. Her red hair was slightly out of place from the frantic afternoon, and her yellow dress had been marked with oven grease. She started to fix her collar and she quickly untied and fixed her apron so it was on straight.

"You're right. I'm sorry." She said in a cold tone. "I am out of line, and I apologize."

"Thank you, dear." Martin pulled down the scarf around his nose to show his wife that he was smiling. "Now, let's do something about that smell. Should I go downstairs to see if there is something wrong with our gas unit?"

She pointed to the door to the basement. "Bradley and I tried, but no such luck. It's hard to believe that a little oven backfire could make the entire house shift."

He too was confused that the house could be affected by something so seemingly insignificant. Martin walked over to the basement door and pulled, but it wouldn't budge at all. "I'll call Henry right now and see how soon he can get over here."

He made his way back into the great room to find that Bradley had been able to open a number of windows, but some still remained stuck in the closed position. The smell was clearing from the house slightly, but he knew that they would need to mask the scent.

"I will also have one of the maintenance workers check the propane tanks on the east wall. Can we get candles going in every room?" Martin was looking from room to room to find his son. "Bradley?"

He made his way to the dining room in between the kitchen and the great room. Bradley was standing in front of their old unused fireplace. He was glaring directly at the gray paint that was covering a brick mantle. He was still and silent. Martin even wondered if he was breathing.

"Bradley?" Martin said as he walked toward him. He was still and completely silent. "Son, are you ok?" Martin touched his son's shoulder.

Bradley snapped his head back toward Martin like he had been oblivious to him. "Yes, Father?"

"What are you doing, Son? You were just standing there."

"I was opening the windows like you asked." Bradley looked up at this father. "Is that proficient, Father?"

"Yes, Son." He paused and began to smile despite his concern. "Very proficient indeed. Thank you." Martin patted the boy on the shoulder.

The telephone began to ring.

"Should we let your sister know that we have everything under control?" Martin pointed to the staircase.

"Yes, Father."

The father and son began to head upstairs when Sarah came into the room from the kitchen. "Martin, it's David. He said that you're needed at the containment lab."

Martin looked at his watch. *What could he possibly need me for, we just talked? It's not four yet.* "This is why I can't ever get anything done. Such incompetence surrounds me." He muttered.

"Bradley, please go check on your sister and assure her that everything is ok." Martin began to untie the scarf that was around his face.

"Yes, Father." Bradley shook his father's hand and proceeded to head up the stairs with one hand on the railing while his left hand in his pocket.

"Please remove your hand from your pocket, Son," Martin spoke as Bradley stopped and turned. "That's not what a gentleman does. It makes it look like you're hiding something. We don't want to give that appearance, now do we?"

"No, Father." Bradley turned on the step. "I apologize. I promise, there is nothing to hide. It was only an honest mistake."

"Please don't let it happen again." Martin turned from Bradley and toward Sarah who was standing still in the same spot listening to the exchange. He gave her a kiss on the forehead. "My dear, I will see you later this evening."

She smiled and nodded.

Martin proceeded to walk out the door and down the steps where his cart was parked on the beautiful stone driveway. He sat on the seat and looked back at the house. He noticed his daughter standing in her window looking down at him. He started to wave to the child, but she stood there motionless.

He paid no more attention to her and began driving down his long driveway when he noticed people at his gate. He sighed in frustration but kept his facial expression somber. He wondered if people heard the explosion from the oven and were curious as to what was happening at the manor. It was never normal to have your day filled with a series of unfortunate incidents. The death of the medic was bad enough, but an explosion at the Hurd Manor was troubling to those who lived close.

The Mayor and his family lived just outside of the downtown district in one of the city's housing sectors. The Hurd Manor was surrounded by a dozen other Victorian-style houses, each on a half-acre lot. Most of his neighbors were retired men and women. The working class lived in the much less developed, East End.

Martin pulled through his gate to see the many people gathered. Each one had a look of concern on their face.

"Mayor Black, we heard a loud sound coming from the manor. *Please,* do tell us that everything is fine." One of the people spoke up.

Martin stepped out from with cart. The people admired his tall and slender build, and his dark hair. His black blazer covered a white button-down shirt with a dark red tie. He smiled simply and politely as he studied the concerned group.

"Lovely people of Copperline. My wife and I very much appreciate your concern." He nodded as he addressed the crowd. "I assure you that everything is more than fine. It's perfect!" He chuckled slightly and waited for the people to change their countenance from worried faces to smiles. "One of the children accidentally turned the propane on to the oven, and my wife lit the pilot. To her surprise, it backfired slightly. I assure you that everything and everybody is okay!"

He surveyed the crowd to see that not only was everybody pleased, but they nodded in approval and smiled at each other.

"We must see to it that we provide you with a new oven," said one of the older gentlemen. "My son can be of service. He's tradesman within the city."

"No, no. That won't be necessary, but thank you so much for your concern." He held his right hand over his heart. "My wife got the stove back to normal and is making a meal for the family who lost their husband and father today. Let us remember Mark Waters. We, the people of Copperline are blessed to have known Mark and for the service, he provided for us. Let us rise up together as friends and neighbors to come alongside this family. When one of us falls, let us join as one to stand through times of misfortune. I'm always amazed to see how great the people become in adversity. Unity will only make us a better city. This is our chance to show the rest of the country that we can rise above any situation to truly be one nation under God." He held his hand and finger high in the air.

Easy, Martin. They were only talking about your oven, he chuckled at the thought.

The people nodded in agreement.

Martin was pleased to see that he had them eating out of his palm once again. He raised his arms wide. "Today, neighbors, we celebrate the life of such an extraordinary man. Let us always remember those who served this city with everything they were. And let us come alongside those who need us most. That is what makes us neighbors! To neighbors!"

"To neighbors!" All the people said together cheerfully.

"Now please do excuse me. I must return to the citadel to prepare for tonight's Celebration of Life." Both of Martin's hands now over his heart. "I do hope to see all of you there."

Some people clapped, while the rest nodded and waved at the great man. Another man shouted once more, "to neighbors!"

Martin climbed back into his cart and the street cleared as he slowly drove through them. Many of the men held their hand out for him to shake, which he made sure to do, despite how quickly he needed to get back to the downtown sector.

Martin drove on the manicured streets of Copperline en route to the citadel, which was next to the hospital. He always enjoyed the citadel. For him, it was the city's fortress, and he was it's king. The citadel was more than a second home, it was a place that he preferred even over his house. A place where all the government officials met. A place of perfect order. A place of spectacular beauty and incredible craftsmanship. One telephone call to David to see just exactly what he was getting into to before he placed himself in any potential danger in the containment lab.

— C —

Martin promptly arrived at his office. Maria greeted him as she usually did with her playfully flirtatious banter. He simply nodded and entered his office. He shut and locked the door behind him. The Mayor sat at his desk and sighed.

He felt under the desk where he taped a key to the surface of the wood. He slowly peeled on side of the tape just enough to grab the key. He unlocked and pulled open a drawer from his desk. The drawer contained only a firearm; a 9mm pistol. Not even the chief guard owned one. They had banned them almost twenty years ago when his grandfather, James Hurd was the acting mayor until his death eleven years ago. To Martin's knowledge, this was the only one in the city.

He hadn't shot one in years and wondered if he'd still know how to use it.

He reached his hand into the drawer and touched the cold metal and instantly remembered the words of his grandfather, "this is only a last line of defense, son. You must never allow yourself to get to the point where this is necessary. Your greatest line of defense is your mind and self control."

Martin spoke softly to himself as he remembered his grandfather. "They say your spirit still lives on in Copperline, but I will silence you. You were much too soft, old man." He chuckled to himself as he began to pick it up. "However, let us just assess the situation first." He rested the gun carefully back in its place as he shut and locked the drawer. He picked up his desk phone and dialed David's extension.

Silence.

He dialed again.

This time a ring, then back to dial tone.

What is this?

Martin put the phone back in its holding place and picked up the receiver again while he held it to his ear and dialed. He listened to the tone of each key as he pressed each number.

Dial tone.

"Why?" He pounded his fist against the wooden desk.

He hit his assistant's extension.

"I knew you couldn't stay away." Maria immediately answered.

"Maria, please. Is there something wrong with the phones today, or am I forgetting the extension to Dr. David Jacobs."

"Dr. Jacob's extension is 2743, Mayor," Maria said.

"Okay. Thank you, Maria. I must've hit a wrong digit. I'll try again." Martin hung up the phone before Maria had the chance to reply.

He dialed the extension again, focusing on making sure he hit each digit correctly. 2 - 7 - 4 - 3.

Dial tone.

He slammed the receiver into the phone and stood from his desk. He stormed over to the office door. Knowing Maria was just on the other side of the wall he calmed himself down and walked through the door.

"Maria, it's probably just a faulty connection somewhere, but I *still* cannot get ahold of Dr. Jacobs," Martin said in a gentle tone. "Would you be able to call the closest maintenance person to look into the grid connector at the telephone facility?"

"I will sir, and I'm terribly sorry for your inconvenience." Maria smiled as Martin started to walk away.

"Thank you."

Martin walked to the courtyard where he would use a private door that was only accessible for authorized personnel. This door led to an underground route that only some government leaders could use. This created an easy and quiet route with minimal distractions to get to different buildings in the city center. Martin liked to refer to this underground tunnel as the subway.

Martin walked briskly through the tunnels. Only the sound of his own shoes against the black granite floor filled his ears.

With the lab corridor just ahead, he began to notice the same familiar smell that was in his house earlier. Martin slowed his pace considerably and became very nervous. *Not now. Not yet,* he thought.

Punching in a code to unlock the door that led to the lobby, Martin cleared his throat and straightened his tie.

That spec, Martin thought to himself. *Why this one?*

Walking through the corridor, he approached the door leading into the main lobby of the lab. He punched another code and entered into the lobby. He took the elevators to one of the hospital's private labs, known as containment.

Containment was usually only for test subjects that became unruly. However, there were a few times when the alchemists' serum made a number of specs go insane and start exhibiting zombie-like symptoms. Those specs were quickly taken care of, and the problems were solved with an airborne virus that killed all the patients inside the confined room. The council members agreed that citizens of Copperline would never need to know they could have had a potential zombie breakout.

As soon as he walked inside, he was greeted by one of the lab workers. "Mayor! Please, this way. David is excepting you."

"Thank you. And what is happening?" Martin said as he walked next to the woman.

"I'm not sure, sir." She said. "Dr. Jacobs only instructed me only to bring you to him."

What do you know? The doctor is capable of making a wise decision on his own, he thought. "What's your name, my dear?" asked Martin.

"Rayne." The woman said as she stopped and held out her hand as an offer to shake his.

"Rayne. I like that name. It's lovely to have met you today, Rayne. You must have parents who are artisans?" Martin smiled and stopped as well and shook her hand.

His smile had a way of capturing people's attention and making them fall for him, and he knew it.

She couldn't help but return the smile and blush ever so slightly. "They are. My mother is a retired painter, and my father was a poet. That's quite the keen observation, Mayor."

"Just an assumption. It's a creative name." Martin said as she began to open the door to the containment area. "Please let me get that," he said as he opened the door.

"This is where my path stops. I don't have clearance to enter there," she said.

"Good answer." He winked at her. "Well, Rayne, it was very nice to meet you today." He smiled and looked into her eyes. "Thank you so much for your hospitality."

"Likewise, Mayor." She said as he entered into the containment lab.

Martin entered the room and waited for the door to be closed before acknowledging David who had been impatiently waiting for him.

"What took you so long?" David was clearly frustrated.

"Maintaining order and perfection. That's what I do around here!" He snapped at David. "Why don't we have a passcode lock on that door? Someday, that's going to come back and bite us, David."

The doctor nodded. "I'll have one installed. We rarely use this r…"

"Why would you call me down here when we had planned to talk later?" Martin asked as he stopped himself. He started examining the melee inside the confined room. "What happened here anyway?" Martin paused as he walked up to the broken glass to see nurses tending to a man with defibrillator paddles grafted into his hands. The room was in utter chaos.

"This happened, sir." David pointed.

"*That* doesn't answer anything! This glass is three inches thick, and it's cracked?" Martin studied the cracks. "Why does that man have defibrillator paddles burned into his hands?"

"Honestly, Martin, I don't even know how that man is still alive. I don't know how any of them are still alive. I've only seen levels like this once before…"

"What happened to the spec?" Martin interpreted him, purposely trying to irritate the older man.

David held up a syringe. "About 4mg of Phenylbutazone."

"But how did it get to this point? Didn't you have him strapped down?" Martin pointed to a hospital bed that was on its side against a concrete wall within the containment.

"He broke out of them and started to go crazy while he was unconscious," David explained.

David's words were tough for Martin to wrap his mind around. *If a spec who was unconscious did this much damage, what is it capable when it's conscious?*

"How long will that put the spec out for?" Martin asked.

David smiled. "It will put a cow out for about 24 hours."

"Is this *funny* to you?" Martin raised his voice. "I get a call from you at my home because something went out of *your* control." He inhaled deep. "You need me down here to fix it? I'm seeing the mess it made all because it's exhibiting supernatural behaviors. Do we have some kind of mutant on our hands? Is this funny?"

"Look, Martin…"

"Don't!" Martin interrupted David. "Figure out what happened to him at that tree!"

"I tried, but that's when he lost it."

Martin glared into him and drove his finger into David's chest. "You came at the spec with the serum, didn't you? It reacted to the threat. I told you *not* to do that. These specs have been shot up their whole pathetic lives, obviously, it's going to be threatened."

"Because you knew this would happen, Martin?" David pushed Martin's hand away. "None of us were ready for this to happen.

Something happened to him inside and we have to figure out before he figures out for himself."

Martin said nothing, but swung his gaze and looked intently into the containment room. He raised his hand to cover his eyes as he shook his head. "Keep the spec in stasis for as long as you possibly can, until we can figure this out. In the meantime, you and I better make sure no news gets out. Can you trust those nurses?"

"I honestly don't know." David looked at the nurses still trying to administer health to the man who was clearly screaming in pain, but the soundproofing was preventing Martin and David from hearing him. "I've listened to them talk. They're trying to wrap their minds around it. Some of them think it's a monster. That's why I'm not planning on letting them out."

"Do they have families that will know they're missing?" asked Martin.

"Only one. The rest are med students with families in other parts of the U.S. I checked up on them before you arrived." David pointed to a nurse in the corner of the room crying and grabbing her ankles looking away from everything happening within the room. "That's her. The one with family here."

"Give her Scopolamine, and start persuading her of the things we need her to believe," Martin said to David who nodded. "I'll contact her family and inform them she is on special assignment. How long until you can have her completely brainwashed?"

"Probably by morning," David said as he looked at his watch.

Martin scowled. "Probably?"

"By morning," David assured him.

Martin focused in on the nurses inside the room. "We don't have enough time to do that to all of them. What do you propose we do with the rest of them?"

David looked up and raised his eyebrows. "Kill them?"

Five

"Today, we celebrate the life of Mark Waters." Reverend Lee McCormick spoke into his microphone as he stood on the steps of the citadel. In front of him, on a wooden platform was an urn that contained the ashes of Mark Waters. Also in front of him were hundreds of Copperline residents joined to remember Mark.

The entire city always shut down out of respect for the individual they were celebrating. Most people would usually watch from their homes on CTV, but there were always the residents who lived closer to the downtown sector that chose to attend in the city square.

"Beloved husband and father, and a devoted medic." The reverend read verbatim from what had been approved by the council. "Copperline was a better place due to Mark's service as a first responder and dedication to preserving the beauty of our beloved city."

Mellissa, Mark's widow stood silently in a black dress while her children stood at her side. Mark Jr. was to her right, and Jordy stood to her left. Mark Jr. was the same build as his father. He was shorter than most men, but still taller than his mother. Jordy was younger than her brother by two years. She was a very intelligent student and an incredible athlete. Jordy was quiet, but very attentive and observant. She and Mark Jr. were both top students at Copperline High.

Jordy had aspirations to enter the medical field like her father. Mark Sr. was a medic, but he was attending university at night to fulfill his dream of becoming a surgeon. Jordy got her determination and work ethic from him.

Mark Jr. planned on going right into the political science training program that the city offered high school graduates. He, like many other young men in Copperline, idolized Martin Black.

Martin decided after the passing of his grandfather to stop referring these moments as funerals. He felt that the word funeral gave people a negative feeling, and in his efforts to try to maintain a positive outlook within the city, he motioned that the funerals be referred to as a celebration of life.

The family would receive Mark's pension, and since he was a city worker his pension was very substantial. Mellissa would be set for life as long as she resided in Copperline.

The reverend continued to speak as his microphone echoed throughout the city square. "Mark and Mellissa moved to Copperline 22 years ago when Mark was accepted into the hospital's medical training program. They have been proper and faithful residents ever since."

"Mark maintained an incredible relationship with his wife Mellissa." Some people smiled as they listened to the reverend speak, while some politely stood quietly holding their hands behind their backs. Mellissa and her children stood there trying to avoid the sympathetic looks of others. Mellissa was the youngest widow ever to lose a husband in Copperline's history. The next closest was, the now passed Edna Marie Earl who lost her husband when she was 45 years old. Fredrick Earl was a utility worker who accidentally fell while working on the expansion at the east side of town.

Tears fell from Mellissa's eyes as the reverend's words carried through the crowded city square. The reverend was right, her and Mark's relationship was strong and didn't necessarily follow the same emotionless pattern as many of her neighbors. Mark and Mellissa agreed that they would play by Copperlin's rules. However, they remained open-minded about many city issues. They always remained true to their faith in the Maker, and in each other.

Mellissa was hesitant about moving to Copperline, but agreed that it was an incredible city with such an incredible opportunity for her husband. Mellissa, like many other wives in Copperline decided to become a stay at home mom and instead of taking a full-time career. She volunteered at the elementary school as much as she could. She began her volunteer work when both of her children were younger, but she had became a part of the culture there. She loved working with younger children.

They both were well respected individuals within their community. Per his time in the military, Mark had been trained in Morse Code, which he taught to his family. It was Mellissa that would practice it with him when he wanted to tell her things that he learned about the city.

He tried explaining details to her that she didn't fully understand about children who were taken from their families at birth and raised in testing facilities. He told her how the government was covering up certain stories to protect the order of the city.

Mellissa thought most of the time he was speculating because it seemed too much to believe and perhaps he was a conspiracy theorist. She wondered if her husband had just received faulty information because of the depth of the accusations. However, she trusted him.

Mellissa would wonder if the stories about the outside world seemed too embellished. She knew that the citizens were terrified of poverty, crime, and poor educational systems. The Copperline media always portrayed the rest of the U.S. as a dying nation.

She always wondered if greed turned people on to Copperline, and fear kept them from leaving.

Then Mark died. Suddenly, and without warning. Apparently in a training incident. All of this happened so fast and Mellissa hadn't even had the time to process it completely. She did sense something odd about the Mayor when he was visiting that afternoon in the hospital. Mark Jr. may have been in his glory, but her intuition was telling her that something was not right with that man.

The officer that was reported at the scene of Mark's death was one that Mark always described as a loose cannon. He was young and full of angst, she remembered him saying.

Mark would beg Mellissa, sometimes in tears to not let any of his information out. He knew how much was at stake, but he trusted his wife. They would surely get removed from Copperline for causing such madness.

Every year people were evicted. Some because families wanted to grow and didn't comply with the two children rule. Others would be asked to leave because they were too vocal in their religious, political, or personal beliefs.

"But as one city, neighbor to neighbor becoming one family, we surround this tribe with our love and support." The reverend covered his heart with his right hand. "We, together as one Copperline. To neighbors!"

The crowd repeated, "to neighbors!"

That struck Mellissa. Never had she been in this position at a celebration of life, and maybe it was purely that, but she never realized how shallow it all was. *Almost cultic,* she thought. And she never liked that the residents had to sign an agreement to be cremated upon passing. A graveyard represented death, and Copperline was to represent a better life. She cried as she thought of how disgusting this all was to her.

After the reverend finished speaking, as a custom, a string quartet plays what is known as the 'Life Medley.' Once the medley was complete, it became evening as usual. People returned to their regularly scheduled nights. The market reopened and the family of the celebrated retired to their home and was allowed one evening of passing.

The evening of passing, she thought. *How am I going to get rid of all his things?* She was glad that she was allowed to keep a few items to remember her husband, but the rest had to be taken and thrown into an incinerator. This was the city's way to move on.

The evening of passing sent chills down Mellissa's spine. How could she only be allowed one evening to mourn and clear out her beloved's possessions? She barely had any time with him as it was when he was alive. The city worked him many hours without any one of them asking her permission, or wondering what her thoughts were on the matter. When he wasn't on a shift, he was studying to become a surgeon. Mark took every second he could with his family and devoted himself to them while he was home, but that time was few and far between.

The quartet finished the medley, and the people gently applauded. The attendees began to peel off from the event. Family by family would greet one another before clearing out completely. A few of the wives came over to offer their sympathy while their husbands tugged at them to leave.

Then the widows came over to Mellissa to offer their celebration group. Mellissa was sickened by all of it. She could still hardly see herself as a widow, and she especially felt too young to be in that position.

People were shaking hands and talking to her, but she retained nothing. She began to see just how plastic everybody looked and how incredibly fake everything sounded. She could only hear her own words in her head, *what will I do now, Mark?* She had resolved at that moment, that she would begin the process of leaving Copperline. Her son would be a hard sell because he had plans in the city, but she knew that there was no future for her here. She hoped Jordy would be on board as well.

"Mother?" Mellissa realized Mark Jr. was nudging her and attempting to get her attention. "Mother! Mayor, Black."

"Yes, Mayor. I'm sorry." She stuttered.

She was always set back by the cologne the mayor wore. Most women found it enchanting, but she was always repelled by the fragrance. There was some lingering musk that made it so offensive to her. Not a very masculine fragrance at all, but she knew he must have had some sort of pheromone-induced potion that the alchemists designed for him alone.

"Please, no need to be sorry." He offered a smile. His wife Sarah was hanging off his arm offering a polite and sympathetic smile as well. "We would love to have you and your family for dinner tomorrow night. Would you accept this invitation?"

Mellissa wanted to shout obscenities, but she didn't know what she would yell at such a time as this. She wanted to punch him, for some reason that was unknown to her. *I don't know why, Mayor, but I'd love to hit you between the eyes.* She wanted to run. She wanted to take Mark's ashes and try to piece them together again just so she could see him and hold him one more time. She was desperate for her husband to return to her. She felt like this was all just a practical joke and Mark would pop out from behind a curtain somewhere with a silly look on his face. The last thing she wanted to do was to have dinner with the Mayor and his plastic wife.

"Mother, please don't let the Mayor wait for a response." Mark Jr. said nudging his mother.

"Sir, I'm sorry. This is just a lot to take in, and I don't want to do or say anything out of order. Please forgive me." Mellissa said with tears falling down her cheeks. She was trying to hold those tears in for fear that they were unacceptable since the quartet was finished, and Mark Jr. seemed to be doing just fine.

Martin reached out his hand and touched Mellissa's chin, which took her by surprise. "Ma'am, please do not feel that you have to apologize. My wife and I just want to bless you and your family."

Red hot fury rose up in Mellissa when he touched her chin. She now felt that she had every reason and good intention to punch this man. *He crossed a line. If Mark were here, he...* She wanted to laugh hysterically and cry uncontrollably, but she restrained herself. She only stood there as slow, pathetic tears crept down her cheek and dropped from her chin to the stone citadel stairs where she had been standing all this time.

"That will be fine. Thank you for your kindness." She forced through more tears. Mark would've wanted her to play along. But she was going to start the process of moving out as soon as next week, she convinced herself. She no longer had Mark there to try to convince her otherwise. However, she would miss those arguments, that somehow Mark always won.

"Mayor Black, I'm looking forward to seeing you tomorrow evening." Mark Jr. was reaching out his hand eager for the mayor to shake it.

Martin shook Mark Jr.'s hand while maintaining eye contact with Mellissa. Sarah offered her condolences and began to recite the menu for tomorrow evening's dinner.

"I'll make a duck a l'Orange with asparagus and roasted red potatoes," Sarah said in a chipper tone with a fake smile.

Martin then directed his gaze toward Jordy. "And Jordy, I'd love to talk with you more. You're very quiet. I understand that you also want to be trained in the medical field."

Jordy smiled and nodded. "Yes sir, I would love to become a neurosurgeon."

Martin smile. "With academic scores like yours and considering your father's affinity for the medical field, that shouldn't be a problem. Copperline has the greatest medical training program in the country. I'm also a personal friend of Dr. David Jacobs who would be interested in knowing that you want to follow in your father's footsteps."

"Thank you, sir!" Jordy maintained eye contact with the mayor, but Mellissa could tell that she was miles away in her head remembering the moments she and her father shared. Smiles and laughter were very common when those two were together.

The mayor had his way of deceiving people to love him even more, but Mellissa wouldn't be fooled. There was something about his stare that she thought was strange. She didn't get carried away by his handsome appearance or his thick charm. She was beginning to wonder if he could somehow read what she was thinking by how intently he seemed to stare into her eyes. It made her very uncomfortable, and she could see that his wife had to be uncomfortable with it as well.

"Have a pleasant evening, Waters family," Martin said as he and his wife walked away.

"To neighbors!" Mark Jr. said in one last effort to gain Martin's attention.

Martin stopped and looked back at Mark Jr. "To neighbors, Mark. To Copperline." With one more smile and look at Mellissa.

— C —

Later that evening, Mellissa was going through Mark's belongings. She would find herself wailing into a pillow so nobody would hear her. The last thing she needed was one of her neighbors reporting her or even worse, showing up at her doorstep for a visit.

She was quite emotional with all of this. She longed deeply for just one last moment with her husband. *Just one more kiss,* she begged Maker.

She found pictures in an album of their wedding and anniversaries. She cried over photos of Mark playing with the children. She smiled at his acceptance letters into the Copperline Medical training program. It seemed like hundreds of thousands of memories laid out in front of her taunting her. She would smell every article of clothing he owned until every last bit of his scent had been removed.

Going through all the books he would read endlessly and prize above any other material possession, she thumbed through pages of his own added notes in the margins. She even found his old Hebrew/English Old Testament Bible which he had to keep in secret. Only religious leaders were allowed to have actual copies of the Bible. People in Copperline were given a paraphrased copy. Mark never felt right about it, so he secretly held on to his. He explained how their paraphrased copy was leaving out bits and pieces of the ancient text.

She laughed as some of the notes in the margins very much indicative of his playful and kind nature. His character was good and everybody knew him to be that way. Mark Waters Sr. was a man of integrity and kindness. He was very loving to his neighbors and cooperative with his colleagues, and always proud of his family.

She turned a few more pages and noticed a small piece of paper sticking out beyond the Bible pages. She pulled it out and examined it.

> *Mark - I can't thank you enough for lending me your books. I have no other way to learn other than what you give me. I want to learn more about Elohim. He seems to fill people with hope. I need hope. I feel like we are going to die in this dormitory. The guard trainees have their way out, but the specs are just waiting for the next fear treatment that will eventually kill us. I'm pretty sure that X is going to kill me if I try to escape again. Sometimes I wonder if that is a bad thing. I'd rather be dead, living with Elohim in the afterlife than getting tested down here. Did Elohim really create us? If he did, do you think he is making me go through this for some other purpose? Is my purpose to be a spec? Mark, thank you for your friendship. You also give me hope.   -spec1982*

Mellissa remembered the conversations she had with Mark. He used to smuggle in books for a few specs. He talked about this one spec in particular, that was extremely well read and good natured. He gravitated toward him especially. She always thought that he shouldn't risk spending too much time with them since it would inevitably get him in trouble.

Mellissa then started to go through books to see if there were any other notes from any of the specs. *There had to be more.* She wanted to see for herself maybe some of the things that Mark told her about. She wondered if there could be some evidence that could be used against the city to set these children free. She began picturing the children that she often worked with at the school.

She frantically took apart boxes and boxes of books. Finally, one note tucked inside the novel, 'The Giver,' which was on Copperline's list of banned reading.

> *Mellissa, if anything happens to me… clean out my locker before they do… I love you more than anything in this world! -Mark*

Her hands began shaking. Her breath was pulled from her lungs. Her head starting spinning. It hit her. Something must've happened, and Mark expected that it may.

"Oh God, no." She stammered and began crying. "Oh, Mark. What do I do?"

She tried to put herself back together. Then she remembered that there could be surveillance watching her right then. She had to be careful about what she said and how she acted. She suddenly felt claustrophobic. She packed up everything back in the boxes, but she knew there had to have been more books. *His locker. I have to get to his locker.*

She only had a few more hours until she wasn't allowed to talk anymore in depth about her passed husband, so she knew she had a limited window to get to that locker. She was frantic now as thoughts slammed through her head as she saw the letter of her husband warning her.

In the kitchen, she looked in the city directory for the extension to the hospital where Mark worked. She grabbed the phone while looking at the clock. She dialed the extension.

Dial tone.

"Come on. Please push me through." She said to herself. She dialed again. "Maker, help me."

The phone rang twice before an answer. "Lab, this is Rayne."

"I'm sorry to bother you. This is Mellissa Waters, Mark's wife." She paused. It felt strange to hear her say those words. Her eyes started to water again, but she fought it as hard as she could. "I was wondering if I could come in and get Mark's belongings out of his locker."

"Actually, no need to worry!" Rayne politely spoke. "The Mayor said he would take care of it tonight. He said he would deliver the contents of the locker to you."

Mellissa slammed the phone down and sprinted across the room for her cart key. Not evening knowing what she was about to do, she threw a steak knife and a can of insect repellent into her purse. She had no plans to hurt anyone, but she feared that she might need them for self-defense.

Mark and Jordy were both in their rooms. With a blue dry-erase marker on the family's to-do list, she wrote "Mark, I'll be right back!! -Mom"

I've got to get there before he does. If he sees anything. What would he see? I don't even know what I'm looking for.

She reached for the doorknob and pulled the door open. She started to walk out the door with her head down, when she abruptly ran into something.

Mellissa looked up to see a tall, dark-haired man. "Going somewhere?" Mayor Martin Black asked.

Six

Stillness.

Where am I?

Silence

"Daniel." I heard what sounded like a chorus of voices. I could see only the surface below me, which looked like a dark blue marble floor. I couldn't see my feet. I couldn't see any part of me, but I was moving through this void.

Am I dead? Did they finally kill me?

I tried to speak, but I couldn't. The only sense that I seemed to be able to use was my vision. I saw a gate attached to a large wall. As I moved closer to the image, I could see an inscription on a plaque of the gate. It read "Copperline - West Gate." It was a large golden plaque.

I had never physically seen much of Copperline, other than the times trying to escape. I could see the craftsmanship and the attention to detail of how the brick was laid on the wall that was connected to the gate. I saw the intricate design of the letters as I moved closer to see the inscription on the plaque in front of me.

I studied the bricks. They weren't red like the clay bricks on the outside of the hospital or cement like the larger bricks in the dorms. These bricks were glossy. They had a design in the stone, almost like marble, but it glimmered like quartz. There were also dark bricks edging out the large C on either side of the gate. I assumed the black bricks had to be obsidian. The metal that made up the giant letter C looked as I imagined platinum would. I'd never seen platinum in my life, but I read about it.

It was so beautiful. I wondered what the meaning of this dream was. *Maybe this is what happens before I die? Maybe I already died.*

I wondered if they had put me in another medically induced coma. It was a terrible thought, but I knew that my body was used to having a cocktail of bad alchemy, so what was a little more? I was a test dummy, and I wasn't given a choice in the matter.

I couldn't help but wonder if I was about to die. I've never had visions like this before.

Either way, whatever was happening to me, it wasn't all that bad. I couldn't feel anything or smell anything. I heard the voices a minute ago, but it became silent again.

As I moved closer toward the gate, it opened for me and I moved inside. Blue fog cleared from my vision and I could see the surroundings. There were no people. No carts. No manicured streets or million dollar homes. There was no world-renowned country club. No community swimming pools or tennis courts. There were none of the large palm trees or tall buildings. There were no red pines or singing birds to sit upon their branches.

It looked like a ghost town. Nothing but old run down wooden buildings with broken windows. Dusty, dirt roads cut out from brown grass that looked very wilted from years of neglect. The buildings were leaning and falling apart.

It was very different from the outside of the gate which was very beautiful and full of incredible designs. This surely didn't seem like the Copperline I'd been told about. I didn't see any glossy black obsidian anywhere. I couldn't see blue marble floors. I only saw something like a city that had been destroyed, maybe years ago. Dust had overtaken everything.

An old wooden schoolhouse stood in the center of the town. I started to enter the schoolhouse, but it was empty. It was nothing but dried up wood and dust.

Outside of the schoolhouse, I saw a sign with ghostwriting that faintly read "Bodie est. 1876" on wood that appeared to be split and dried from the sun.

Was this before Copperline? I remembered reading in one of the books that Mark let me borrow of a place called Bodie, California. *What about this place was so desirable? What happened here?*

I made my way through the abandoned ghost town. *Why, of all the things that I could dream about, am I dreaming about this place?*

"Are you dreaming?" A voice spoke out of the stillness around me. I heard it again, but almost in a whisper, "what are you dreaming of?"

I wanted to speak, but I couldn't get my voice to become audible. It was as if I was mute. The sensation and the ability to speak were nonexistent.

Why can't I tell where your voice is coming from? Where are you?

"Daniel, open your eyes." The angelic voices called out.

I am. My eyes are open. I can see.

"No, Daniel. Open the eyes to the man inside of you. See with your heart."

I don't know what that means. Am I Daniel?

"Yes, Daniel. You must not walk by what you can perceive with your physical eyes, but you need to see with the heart."

See with my heart? That doesn't make sense. It only makes me question more. Where are you?

"I'm inside you," the voices said.

How?

"I've always been inside you," the voices laughed together in unity.

But I didn't know. Why is this happening?

"What do you see?" The voices became louder as if they were right in my ears now. I could feel a slight breeze on my skin. I could sense my physical body again.

I see an old town full of dust and rubble. What happened here? I studied the ground and the buildings to see if there was a hidden meaning somewhere, but I couldn't see anything of significance. I was trying to remember anything I had I read from that book about Bodie. I could remember that it was once a booming town for a short while. A town involved in the gold rush period. *Gold. Pride?*

The slight breeze increased to the point that it filled my ears with swirling noise.

"A town neglected, left for dead?" I was able to speak again. I started to spin around and around looking for something. "There's nothing here! Why did the people leave here? Is this Copperline?

"You got that right, kid." The wind stopped. Stillness. I turned around to see a man wearing an old black top hat and his hands at his side ready to draw out a firearm from the holsters he wore around his belt. The man was close to 60 or 70 yards away. The hat and the clothes he wore were all black, but they were just as tattered as most of the rest of the town. His voice was agitating to me.

Whispers surrounded me. I couldn't understand the language they were speaking, but I was certain that I heard them call me, "Danny. Are you dreaming Danny Boy?"

"Can you see me?" I asked. All my senses were quickly coming back to me. I could feel myself breathing. I felt the hot sun blaring down on my skin.

"I sure can, but you're in my town." He snarled at me as he took two steps closer. When he walked, it looked as if he was moving through the air as a ghost would. *This surely couldn't be the keeper of the voice that I was just talking to.*

"I'm not even here on my own will. I'm dreaming," I said, studying the man in front of me.

"You ain't dreaming, you fool." He took two more steps closer to me. "You need to leave me alone and keep your mouth shut."

"About what?" I raised my hands up. I could also see my body again. My bare feet were touching the ground. I could feel the dry, hard dirt underneath my toes. "Are you the one that's been talking to me? Your voice is different."

"You keep your mouth shut, boy!"He yelled at me. Hundreds of child-like laughs hung in the air. "You're all the same. All you specs! You want to get out. You got a good look at the others who tried to run, didn't you?"

"Specs?" I asked. "What are you doing with them?"

"Tsk, tsk. You ask too many questions."

"Are they alive?" I asked. A thick pungent smell filled the air as he came closer. It reminded me of being in the cave.

"That's right. You saw them specs that time I almost got you. You're remembering it too, aren't you? You'll end up like them if you don't shut your mouth." He stopped walking forward and crossed his arms. "You must have good luck, kid."

"I don't believe in luck. I believe in grace. Luck is for people who are in denial." I studied him. The look of his face sent a shudder through my soul. *What am I looking at anyway? This isn't a human.*

He started laughing. “Grace!” He laughed even more. His mouth opened to a point that I knew was not humanly possible. “Grace! That’s good, kid! That’s really good!”

I became extremely uneasy of whatever this was approaching me. I could now see bone-like tusks coming out of the back of the creature’s head. His skin was reddish and appeared to be scorched. He had tiny spurs all over his hands, like talons from a large bird.

“I actually think… you could work for me. Yeah, I think that would work.” He changed his tone and had a strange look on his face. It was contorted in a way that was much different from a minute ago. He began acting like a marionette. His actions were extremely exaggerated and disturbing.

He took another few steps closer. So close, that the rancid smell of sulfur and stale death started to make me nauseous. That was the smell I remembered from the cave under the tree. He came closer. I noticed that he didn’t have eyes, only empty eye sockets. He opened them wide as he noticed me looking into them.

“Yeah, you and Mayor.” He continued as he chuckled. “The doctor, and a few more of the city council folk.”

“The mayor? Of Copperline?” I asked.

“That’s right, I got him. He was an easy one though. A lot like the people who lived in this town.” He shrugged and snapped his fingers to make a cracking sound that echoed what seemed like a hundred times. The sky darkened in an instant. “I just gave them a little gold, but they all took it and left. Greedy folk.”

“What gold? What do you know about the doctor?” I asked. I stepped back with every step he took toward me.

“I saw the way you looked at him. You know there’s something different. You’ll see it even more in Martin. He’s the ace up my sleeve” He hissed the last words he said. “Oops, I let you in on my little secret.”

He started laughing hysterically, so much so that he closed his eyelids, but when he opened his eyelids again, he had big yellow eyes. “Kid, I can give you the same power that I gave them. You can have whatever you want. I’ve been watching you. I know exactly what you want. You want freedom.”

How could you possibly know what I want. I don’t even know who I am.

His eyes became dark again, but I could see what appeared to be a night sky in his eye sockets. I was drawn into them. I suddenly began to see the thoughts that were in my head within his eyes. When he said freedom, I saw myself with a family, a brother, and sister. I could see my mother. The song that the nurse was humming was in the air around me as the sky became as black as night.

Child-like whispers all around me filled the sky. “Danny Boy, come play with us."

“Yeah, that’s right, kid.” He snarled and flicked his tongue on his teeth like a snake. His teeth were yellow and brown, but curled and sharp. “You’ve been living in poverty for too long and you don’t even know what’s available. What about wealth?”

A picture filled his eyes of me living in a large house. I was wearing clean clothes. I was enjoying a drink while I looked out at a beautiful vineyard.

“I bet it gets real lonely being a spec and all. You must want the companionship and intimacy.” He flicked his snake-like tongue again, but I was too enamored by the vision that I couldn’t take my eyes off of his. “Yeah. Don’t ya kid?”

The sky now became filled with the image of a wedding. I was smiling. I was holding someone’s hand. There were people surrounding us with joyful expressions. I looked peaceful. I looked happy. I looked like how I would imagine one of the residents looking. I glared at the sky.

I think he's right. I do want all of it. I want to know what it feels like to be free. I want to know what love is. I don't want to be a test dummy anymore. I felt like I was going to burst into tears.

"Kid, it's yours if you want it." When he spoke, the sky became black with not even as much as a star to fill it.

"No, bring the vision back!" I searched frantically in the sky around me. "Let me see more!"

"Just bow down to me."

Whispers followed by laughter surrounded me again from every direction. It sounded like children saying, "bow down, Danny Boy."

The man with the hat stood there silently as if he was awaiting my response.

"Daniel." Suddenly the deep, angelic voices returned from before the man appeared. Such a contrast, but also a mystery. I turned my head to try to find where the voices were coming from, but I could only see the man with the hat looking back at me. "Daniel, he can't hear me. Only you can right now. Don't be fooled by him. That man has come to kill, destroy and divide."

I stood silent. The man in the hat came another step closer. He could see that I was agitated and startled by something. "Well, kid?"

"Daniel, remember what you know in your heart. I have set you apart as a chosen instrument to bring them the truth." The voices called out to me.

"What do I do?" I asked as I frantically tried to find where the voice was coming from.

The man stopped. His eyes became orange, like fire. "He's here, isn't he? He's talking to you isn't he?" He looked around and then snapped his head back at me. "Kid, just come to me. Now."

The ground started to shake. Dust began swirling everywhere around me. In the distance, it looked like the world was crumbling to pieces from the ground up to the sky. The horizon started to turn in toward me as what I would imagine a tidal wave to look like. Soon, I could see the mountains that were once in the distance were curling up above me. Everything was warping and inverting.

"Daniel, run to me!" The deep, angelic voices called out.

The man with the hat stood and started laughing. His face started to burn with an orange fire as he looked at the sky and started to scream. The scream sounded like a siren. It was so loud that it was making me physically ill.

"All this will stop if you just bow to me, Danny Boy!" The man with the hat screamed.

I started running away from the ground as it was crumbling and flipping upside down. "What do I do?" I screamed, but nothing. The piercing sound of the screaming combined with the haunting sound of the earth crumbling was frightening me.

"Elohim!" I cried out at the top of my lungs. "Elohim!"

The dust was catching up to me. I couldn't run fast enough to escape the chaos around me.

Rocks and large pieces of earth began dropping like boulders all around me.

"Elohim!" I screamed. I ran.

Something was changing on the horizon. The ground came to an end. I watched the dirt and dust fall off the end of the earth like a waterfall as it disintegrate into nothing. I couldn't see any more land in front of me. All I could make out was a bright and blinding light making everything white. As soon as I got to the edge of the earth, something told me to jump. I began to fall with my arms swinging all around as if I were a newborn bird trying to fly for the first time. I was falling into nothingness.

Why did I jump? What am I doing?

"Elohim!" I let out one more cry that emptied my lungs of everything I had left. My voice was strained but loud. I could hear it echo into the vast, white nothing in front of me. Dozens of angelic voices started to respond to me as they all sang, "Elohim!"

Then suddenly, without warning and beyond my capability to understand how, I landed. I landed on one knee with two hands catching my fall, but there was no foreseeable ground underneath me. I brought myself to my feet to see that I was standing on nothing. It was white all around me. I could only see my body surrounded by white light. I wasn't hurt, just confused at all of this.

I could no longer hear the sound of the earth collapsing and folding in on itself above me. I heard a faint sound that was much more pleasant. It reminded me of the binaural music the doctors would have us listen to when we were loaded with meds, but this was much more preferable. The sound was ethereal. It didn't sound like the music was coming from instruments but it was somehow flowing out of the air moving around me.

I walked around in my bare feet with my arms out, trying to feel for a wall or something that would give me bearings as to where I was. Everything looked the same.

Small streams of light wrapped around me as I walked. Fog was beginning to form all around me and I could see that the light was emitting from the fog.

I felt warm as I reached out to touch it. I felt peaceful, maybe for the first time ever. It was incredible and terrifying all at the same time. I couldn't wrap my mind around it, so I decided to just remain in it. I imagined it to be like I was basking in an evening golden hour on a warm summer afternoon, something that I've only seen from a tiny window.

"Daniel, I created you for such a time as this." One deep voice surprised me and it echoed through the air. As the voice spoke the fog flashed like lightening.

The air around me was still vibrating with the heavenly sound all around me. I started to smell a wonderful fragrance. It was unlike anything I had smelled before. I was trying to breathe in as much of it as possible. It was almost as if I was instantly addicted to the floral smell. I reached for the fog and felt its warmth with my fingers. It brought a greenish-blue hue to the white void as I touched it. It was a mesmerizing. I laughed audibly and I could hear the echo return to me as a child's laugh from every direction.

I was glad to be away from the man with the hat. I never wanted to see him again.

"Elohim?" I asked. "Is this the afterlife?"

Only the slight sound or the air filled my ears. I started to become more confused as to why I was there. That made me anxious.

"Why aren't you listening to me?" I called out and listened to my childlike echo back at me. "What was I created for?"

"Bring the truth to them. Truth will set them free."

"What is truth?" I asked.

"The truth that is within love."

Seven

"Mayor Black, I… I…" Mellissa stammered out.

"I know," he said as he bowed his head almost as if he were ashamed. "I should've called first, but I knew you would probably want this since tonight is the evening of passing." Martin stood holding the box with the hospital logo on it.

Mellissa questioned his intentions but received the box from Martin nonetheless. "Thank you, Mayor, that's very generous of you."

"Please, no thanks needed. I am here to serve the people of Copperline. To neighbors, right?" He motioned behind him. "This is my son, Bradley. Bradley, this is Mrs. Waters."

"Pleased to meet you, Bradley." Mellissa politely offered her hand to shake.

"Good to meet you, ma'am. I'm sorry about your husband." Bradley shook her hand and smiled.

Mellissa set the box down on the floor in the foyer. "I really do appreciate the kind gesture, and I apologize if I seemed distant at the celebration this evening. It's all happened so fast."

"Mellissa, I understand." His voice became soft and soothing. "When I lost my grandfather, I was a lost soul, and it took more than one evening to get over it."

Mellissa started to think she might have been wrong about him. She wondered if she was being over dramatic about her husband's passing. However, Mark just died. She felt that she was justified to be angry and confused.

"Look, Mellissa." He paused and looked at Bradley. "Son, please meet me in the cart. I'll be right out."

"Yes, Father," Bradley replied as he turned and walked casually back to the cart. Mellissa thought to herself that the boy's mannerisms were too robotic. It was no doubt that Martin had his son trained very well.

"Mellissa, we…" He grimaced as he spoke, "we have reason to believe that your husband may have had illegal connections at the hospital. Do you have any reason to believe he could've been involved with anything like that?"

There it is. Mellissa stood with a million thoughts running through her mind. *You come here on the evening of passing to accuse my deceased husband of illegal connections?* She quickly reverted back into the angry and discontented attitude that she held against him. *Does he actually know something? Is he just trying to see if I'll talk? Why else would he inconvenience himself and come all the way over to the East End? He has an agenda.*

"I'm sorry?" She asked. Her patience was running thin. "Are you accusing my dead husband of being involved with a conspiracy?"

"Ma'am, please." He held his hands up and spoke to her like a child. "We don't say dead, it's passed."

"I'm sorry, are you accusing my passed husband of involvement with a conspiracy?" She restrained her volume so her children wouldn't hear her. She could feel rage growing within her.

She worried that if he said one more wrong thing, she would attack him. She envisioned herself pushing him through the wall or digging her fingernails into his face. *Mellissa, stop. Where is this coming from?*

"No, ma'am. I'm just finding out about a potential illegal connection within the hospital." He started to smile again. "Look, I'm sorry. My timing is extremely inappropriate. Mark was a fantastic man, and I'm sure this is all an enormous misunderstanding. I mean you and your family no harm or disrespect. We will see you for dinner tomorrow, yes?" He started to walk out of the door as he awaited her response.

In a wave, the scent of his cologne hit her again. She was aggravated by it, but suddenly her rage dissipated and she lost her will to argue.

"Yes. I'm sorry for raising my voice. Again, under the circumstances."

"Yes." He smiled. "Under the circumstances. Goodnight."

She nodded and replied, "goodnight."

— C —

As Martin walked down the sidewalk to his cart, he wondered if she knew something. It was almost like she could read his mind. He wondered if he had said too much and she was on to him, but it was clear that she was just emotionally drained. He did need to find that missing book from Mark's locker that he wrote about in his journal. While he was inside the house, he allowed his eyes to search as much as possible without looking too obvious.

"Father?" Bradley asked, "did you ask her for the book?"

"No, son. Mrs. Waters had a lot on her mind, and I didn't want to burden her with some lost book."

"Why *that* book, Father?" Bradley looked up at Martin.

"No reason that would concern you, Son." Martin smiled and patted Bradley's knee.

Bradley studied everything his father did. Even more than Martin realized. "Father, shouldn't a future mayor have this information?"

Martin silently appreciated his son's enthusiasm and affinity for protecting the order of Copperline. "In due time, Son."

— C —

Mellissa watched Martin walk down her driveway from behind a closed shade. She watched how he walked with robot-like perfect posture. However, she also noticed how he slipped his left hand into his pocket and held it there until stepping into the cart.

That's odd, she thought to herself. She knew that it was improper for a man to walk with one's hand in his pocket. It was one of the unwritten codes of ethics in the city that she thought was preposterous, however, he was breaking one of his own silent laws.

She watched an interaction with his son before they drove off. She was frustrated at how he showed up uninvited in the way that he did. She had a suspicion that he must've gone through the contents of the box and found something.

She started searching through the box. She looked through all the books and searched their pages, but every book was clean. Only tattered pages and a few random messages in the footnotes of several pages.

She got to the bottom of the box and the only thing that remained was an old Copperline Ledger notebook. On the back, Mark had written down an inventory of every book he had in his work locker. Mellissa thought that it was most likely a way he kept tabs on the books he lent out. Every book, but one was accounted for. *'The Art of War'* was missing. Mellissa knew instantly that the book was on the banned reading list for the city. She questioned its absence.

Also inside the ledger was a bunch of small journal entries that were entitled "Dear Mellissa."

Each numbered entry had a code-like letter and number combination at the bottom of the page. The codes read with an AOW followed by a one, two, or three digit number. She immediately assumed that the "AOW" must've referred to the lost book, *'Art of War.'* She also assumed that the number must be pertinent to page numbers.

Reading through each small entry, she would smile and cry. Each word that Mark inscribed would remind her of the man that he was. She tried to hold her focus on the task at hand, which was to find some sort of clue that Mark left her. However, each penned word made her miss him even more than she thought possible. She loved and hated at the same time that he printed every letter like it was a capital letter. She remembered how they would playfully argue about the correct way to write certain letters. She would miss the subtle flirting. He always had a way of making her feel like she was a teenager in love.

Something quickly grabbed her attention when she spotted an anomaly in the journal. While each entry was numbered, the entries jumped from #21 to #23. It looked as if entry #22 had been ripped out. *The mayor.* She shook her head and held her forehead with her hand. She clenched her eyes shut. She became fearful that the mayor had that very entry in his pocket as he was walking away.

She turned to entry #23.

> *"Dear Mellissa-* On pages past, you'll find the clue. You must get to them quick, before they do. *I love you."*

At the bottom of the page, it said "AOW142#*"

She saw the pound sign and asterisk and saw that this was the only entry with a code like this. She remembered that when Mark had to write things in code for the military, they would write numbers for dates and locations by using the symbols that corresponded with each number of a computer keyboard.

However, it had been forever since she used a keyboard. She wondered where she could find one. While the children didn't have any personal computers, the school certainly did, but she would never get into the school at this time of night.

"Jordy!" She said aloud. She knew that Jordy would be very familiar with the keyboard since she used it more than anyone in the family.

She rushed to the stairs and ran up, skipping every other step. Jordy's door was slightly open. Mellissa knocked once, then immediately entered. Her daughter had fallen asleep, most likely from the weariness and exhaustion of the day. Mellissa looked at her daughter's face and the streaks in her makeup from all her tears.

"Jordy," Mellissa whispered while gently nudging her daughter. "Jordy."

Jordy's eyes jolted open. "Mother? Are you… Is everything ok?" She spoke as she sat up against her headboard.

"Yes, honey. I'm just trying to figure out something your father wrote. It's in code." She flipped through the pages to find entry #23. "It's a pound sign and an asterisk. Didn't your father have some number code that pertained to the symbols on a keyboard?"

Jordy grabbed a notepad that was sitting upon the nightstand next to her bed. She started writing out the numbers of the keyboard, one through zero. Then above each number, starting with an exclamation mark, she put the correct corresponding symbol above each one.

“Yes, but they were opposites.” She directed her mother’s attention to the notepad. “If pound sign was three, that means he meant eight. Because counting back three keys from zero would be eight. And an Asterisk would be eight, but the opposite would be three.” She paused to see her mother’s comprehension.

Mellissa sat there thinking. “So you’re saying it means eighty-three?”

“I think so. Father used to leave me messages in code all the time too.” She smiled. “They all equaled different ways to say ‘I love you, Jordan.’ I’m going to miss that.”

Mellissa quickly found entry #83. It was unlike the other entries. There was no “Dear Mellissa.” It only read three small words other than the #83 in the top right corner of the page. On the inside lower corner of the page, Mellissa noticed the words, “GET THE BOOK.”

Mellissa lifted her head and noticed her daughter looking intently at her. She froze.

“Mother?” Jordy sat forward. “What is it?”

— C —

Mellissa started looking everywhere for *‘The Art of War.’* She tore the entire contents of her living room, bedroom, and basement apart. She wondered if Martin had found it and taken it before he gave her the box.

Martin was here because he wants the book. Did he take it? If he did, why would he mention the illegal activity? Was he waiting to see what I would say?

She started to panic. The book was nowhere to be found in the house. Because it was a book that was on a list of unapproved books. She was worried if she or one of the children were caught with it, they would surely be disciplined.

Why would Mark even risk bringing it to work? Mark, what did you have in that book?

Mellissa entered the kitchen and found a clean glass in her cupboard. All of this was giving her an intense headache. She reached for some ibuprofen in a cupboard above the refrigerator. She turned the faucet on and let the water run for a bit to cool the temperature before she filled the cup. Her gaze landed on a picture on the window sill above the sink. The picture was last year's family portrait of the four of them at Hurd Park.

Studying the picture, she reminisced. It was a Sunday after the morning service. The family commonly attended service together, but Mark would always treat them to a big lunch in the park square. They would laugh together and talk about their busy weeks. The children would talk of their big plans for the future while Mark would encourage them. Mellissa just watched and smiled mostly, but her heart was content when the four of them were together.

Tears again began to stream down her face. She slammed the faucet off and took a sip of the crystal clear and cool water. If there was one thing she absolutely loved about Copperline, it was the water. She and Mark grew up in the Northeast. Her old city townhouse in the North End of Boston was beautiful and full of charm, but Boston city water didn't even begin to compare to Copperline's pristine public water. She always had liked the water.

She had been in Copperline all these years because of Mark, but finally, this was her way out. There were too many lies being told, and secrets being harbored. She knew it would be a long and drawn out process, but she knew that her family had to get out of this place. They needed to move out before Mark Jr.'s 18th birthday. Otherwise, he would opt to stay in the city. She wouldn't be able to handle her son becoming part of the mayor's team.

She started to panic again about the missing book. From tears to trembling, she stood there completely paralyzed by fear. She felt her heart rate rise to a point where she could do nothing. She shook her head as she started mumbling to herself, "pull it together, Mellissa."

She took a deep breath and willed herself to calm down. She put the glass down gently on the concrete countertop and stood quietly until she felt herself calm down.

She thought to herself, *where do I look? What is in that book, Mark?* She knew that it was no coincidence the mayor brought the box over. There was no doubt that if he saw it, he had already taken it from the box. She wanted to believe that she could still find it somewhere before the mayor.

Mellissa went over the possibilities. If Martin had it already, she would never know what Mark had for her to know. If the mayor didn't have it yet, he was trying to get information. She concluded, that he couldn't possibly have the book yet. *He was trying to get information out of me, she thought.*

For someone who kept secrets all the time, he was bothered that there was something out there that he didn't have his hands on, she supposed.

I'll make it my mission to find that book before he does.

— C —

Martin and his son arrived at the gate of Hurd Manor. He lifted the cover of the keypad and punched in the 7-digit code. The gate slowly opened.

"Father, when will you give me the code?" Bradley asked.

"I change it frequently." Martin started to push the accelerator to the cart. "We have to protect our home, Son. We can't just allow any unexpected guests into our house. We have to protect our family, but also protect the order of Copperline, first and foremost. There are things that people wouldn't understand."

"Then why are we having the Waters family over for dinner?" Bradley asked.

"We've invited them, and that's okay." He looked at Bradley. "However, uninvited guests are simply not allowed, son."

"To Copperline," Bradley said. Bradley always made a habit of looking his father in his face to see how he responded.

Martin, still looking at his son with no emotion nodded. "Always and only, to Copperline."

The cart came to a stop at the end of the stone driveway. Bradley sprang out of the cart and began jogging up the stone walkway. He entered the house before Martin. Martin reached his left hand in his pocket and pulled out a small piece of paper that read #22 in the top right corner of the page. He studied the words again.

> *Dear Mellissa - If anything happens to me, please make sure to read my copy of the art of war. It's a book, and I've left you notes in the margins. You can't allow the city council to see it. Expose their secrets. - Mark*

Martin scowled at the words written.

What did he have written in there? What was he doing with such a book anyway?

The Mayor was frustrated that a family in the city even had that book in the first place.

An unapproved book was one thing, but leaving notes for the city council not to see, was another. What kind of secrets was he trying to expose? I have to find that book.

"Martin, dear." Martin entered the front door. Sarah stood in the foyer of the house to greet her husband.

"Sarah." He looked at his wife, still with the same emotionless look that he gave his son. He dramatically lifted his nose to smell the air. "Why does it *still* smell? Do you have *any* candles you could burn?"

Sarah smiled politely and motioned to the kitchen counter where there was one candle burning. "Anything else, my dear?" Sarah curtsied as she looked at her husband sarcastically.

"Yes, actually." Martin waited for the door to close and latch, then his volume level instantly increased. "You could cut the sarcastic remarks. I give my all to this town, and this is how you treat me? This is how you take care of our home?"

She looked at him while she clenched her jaw. Her eyes began to water. "I saw the way you touched her chin tonight. You just came from there, didn't you?"

"I was there because Bradley and I returned a box of her husband's belongings to her. I was on the job." Martin brought his voice low again, but he was agitated. "I touched her on the chin because I'm a mayor who knows what his people need. I know what this city needs. This city needs me."

"On the job? Is that what you call it now? Whenever you slip away with your assistant, are you just on the job?" Her voice became loud. "What about *us*, Martin? What about me? Were you even concerned for me today when our stove malfunctioned?"

He remained still and silent, though he was ready to burst. *Not in front of the children,* he said to himself. *You'll regret this, Sarah.*

"No!" She pulled back her volume level again to a suppressed, but forthright tone. "You rushed here because you knew people would question the noise, and you'll do whatever it takes to maintain order in your precious Copperline."

"Woman," he said as he pointed at her. He slowly stepped toward her, one step at a time. "You better watch the way you talk to me." He turned his head away and looked at her out of the corner of his eye. "You will not disrespect us in this house, and you will never question my actions again. My job and my plans to keep order in this city are not pertinent to you."

"But what about me?" She asked.

Martin stepped closer and began to arch over Sarah. He knew that she saw the rage in him. She started to shake ever so slightly.

Sarah kept her face straight ahead and wouldn't make eye contact with him. A single tear streamed down her face from her left eye.

Martin noticed the tear and how it made her makeup run. "Pull yourself together. You look like a mourning widow."

"You would know, wouldn't you." She looked directly into his dark eyes. "Who can resist Mayor Martin Black?" Another tear fell down her cheek.

In an instant, his right hand moved so fast that Sarah never even saw it hit her face. The room was filled with the loud cracking sound of his flesh slamming hers. Martin slapped her so hard with the back of his hand, that it sent Sarah to the floor.

She looked up at him in fearful shock as she backed herself quickly underneath a table in the foyer. He could tell that she knew she pushed him too far.

"Go ahead and cower under the table like a dog!"

"Martin," Sarah whispered. "Not in front of the children."

Martin felt a sense of satisfaction come over him. He lowered his voice again and stared at the back of his hand. "Woman, when will you learn?"

Just then Martin noticed Margret sitting on the top step listening to every word and watching her father assault her mother. He saw that her eyes were filled with tears. He began approaching his daughter. Shaking his head and slightly grinning, he began taking one step after the other up the stairs toward his quivering fear-stricken daughter.

Margret stood and slowly started to back up the stairs with her eyes fixed on the man. He could see the hurt and the betrayal in her eyes.

"Margret, honey," Martin said in a emotionless tone as he cracked neck. "You stop right there and give your father a kiss."

Margret stopped moving backward. With one hand on the oak railing, she slowly made her way to Martin. She stood there softly whimpering.

"Now, that's not very ladylike." Martin tilted his head. "Now give me a kiss on the cheek." Martin leaned down and moved his head closer to her.

Margret slowly leaned in and kissed her father. "Sorry, Father."

"Sometimes when Father does that to Mother, it is only because I love her so much." Martin said into her ear, just above a whisper. "Perhaps someday, I will show you that same kind of affection."

Martin stood straight. He looked down the steps to see that Sarah was slowly starting to get up and make her way into the powder room.

"Now go up into your room, my dear." Martin returned his gaze to his daughter. He brought his voice to a normal volume. "And Margret?"

"Yes, Father?"

"Nobody outside this house quite understands the love that I have for my family." Martin glared at his daughter.

Margret looked back up at her father. "Yes, Father." She turned and quickly entered her room.

Martin made his way back down the steps and stood in front of the powder room door. Raising his hand to knock, he noticed out of the corner of his eye, Bradley standing in front of the dining room fireplace again. Martin had noticed this was becoming a normal, albeit strange occurrence.

“Son?” Martin walked over to Bradley who had no emotion on his face as he stood, looking at the mantle. “Bradley? Son?”

In a small whisper, Bradley said something that Martin didn’t hear. He remained still with his gaze fixed to the wall. It was followed by another whisper that was unclear.

Martin thought he recognized the words, but he couldn’t imagine his son would even know that language.

“What was that, son?” Martin leaned in toward Bradley. “I thought I heard you say…"

“I can hear him,” Bradley whispered again.

“Hear who, Son?” Martin knelt and leaned into the fireplace to see if he could hear. As he knelt, he noticed a floorboard had recently popped up.

Martin felt a slight of cold air coming from the old brick structure.

“The voice.” Bradley said “I told him my name was Bradley. They told me only to whisper in my mind.”

Martin looked at his son. “Get upstairs now and do not leave your room until I tell you.”

“But Father!” The boy made his plea.

Martin stood to his feet and grabbed Bradley by the shirt collar and pulled him away from the fireplace. “Don’t make me do something that is not gentlemanlike to you, Son. Now get upstairs, and do not disrespect me again.”

Bradley turned and quickly walked up the stairs and entered his room.

Martin waited to hear the sound of his door latching shut before he moved. Once he heard the door latch shut, he moved toward the powder room door.

Sarah came out of the powder room. She had fixed her makeup and met her husband with a gentle smile. "Martin, I'm sorry about how I disrespected you in front of our children. Please forgive..."

"There's no time for that. Bradley heard them through the fireplace in the dining room. I'll board it up for tonight. You go upstairs and keep the other two quiet."

— C —

Sarah put a hand over her mouth and nodded. She instantly headed up the steps and into a closet that was locked at the top of the steps. Grabbing a black key from her apron, she unlocked the door. Inside, she looked quickly for duct tape and rope. She picked up her supplies and locked the door.

Hurrying up the stairs to the third floor, the housewife came to another door at the top of the stairs. Sarah pulled out the same black key and slowly unlocked the door. She turned her head to look around to make sure Bradley or Margret didn't see her.

What do I do?

When she saw that she was unnoticed, so she quietly and gently closed the door behind her. She switched on a hanging light and crept her way up the stairs. Her shadow danced back and forth as the hanging light swayed. She listened to the slight creaking of the stairs under her feet as she slowly climbed the old wooden stairs.

— C —

Martin rushed outside to the carriage house where he stored lumber that was left over from a past porch remodel just a few years ago. The wood was rough sawn pine in various lengths. Martin grabbed armfuls of the wood at a time, bringing it into the dining room.

He knew that a hammer and power saw would be too loud at this time of night, and that would cause people to wonder what he was doing. He grabbed a handsaw and a cordless screw gun also from the carriage house.

Inside the manor, he immediately began cutting boards down to lengths that would cover the front of the mantle.

He made himself a frame that he could attach the boards. He knew this would just be a temporary fix until he could get Henry to renovate the space.

Martin sawed away. His brow became sweaty and anger was ubiquitous within him. He was angry at himself, angry at his family, angry at the lack of order in just this past day, and mostly angry at the spec. He was annoyed at the widow and her lack of interest in him. He was infuriated with the lost book somewhere in his city. He was worried that if the book was found, it could potentially bring down everything that he'd been trying to protect all these years.

This is all her fault for having the children. She knew the rules. She's so unsubmissive, he thought as he continued to sweat while he worked hastily.

— C —

Sarah made her way to the top step and slowly turned a doorknob to the attic. She opened the old wooden door and stepped inside, holding the duct tape in one hand and the rope around her other arm. She softly shut the door behind her. *Are they sleeping? How could Bradley hear them if they were sleeping?*

The door closed slowly. The sound of the latch startled them and they turned to see Sarah standing in the dimly lit attic.

"Mommy."

Eight

Dr. David Jacobs looked at a computer monitor showing him results that were unexplainable. He instructed his team to clean up the containment room and get the man whose hands were burned by the defibrillator into a similar secured area. He needed medical attention immediately. David also convinced the nurses that there could be potential danger from being exposed to whatever the spec had. Any possible contraction of a disease or virus was always something they were worried about when dealing with specs.

Martin and David instructed the team of medical personnel to spend the next few days in observation to be cleared of anything harmful. Each nurse agreed it would be the best decision since they, themselves had never witnessed anything of that magnitude.

The alchemists were always busy working with new vaccines to test on intentionally infected specs. Medical research and development teams were making Copperline money by working on secret government contracts. David would market the vaccines and the city would benefit greatly from the sale. Martin saw the potential beyond the walls of the city. He had plans for Washington, and that scared David.

As he stood in thought, David looked past the broken glass into containment room one where the spec was lying unconscious. Now, once again on a new and clean hospital bed. The debris had been cleaned up and removed from the room. The only thing in the room other than the spec on the bed was a single IV. An IV that kept the spec in a medically induced coma.

An alarm on David's watch vibrated. Its notification read, "TB." He looked at the watch, then quickly gazed back at the spec. He nodded at the specimen lying still and proceeded to exit the containment room.

Jacobs, with his hands behind his back, walked past the lobby entrance. He passed several hospital workers and acknowledged several people as he walked. He made his was into a brightly lit hallway that ended with a door to a staircase in front of him, and two elevators to the right. David swiped his badge over a reader shifting his eyes to see if anyone was around him. Waiting for the reader to accept his card, the elevator door moved to reveal an empty space. David entered and hit the button for the 3rd floor. He stood motionless with his hands behind his back waiting for the door to close.

He feared this spec had something about different about him. However, he exhibited similar attributes as Martin. They had comparable characteristics, but the spec's numbers were quite troubling.

The elevator came to a stop. The doors opened to the 3rd floor. David made his way slowly past the receptionist at the desk and down a carpeted hallway. He was always delighted at how different the third floor looked than the rest of the hospital. They intentionally did that to put patients at ease. Warm colors, softer surface to walk on, comfortable waiting room chairs, and better music.

A lot of patients that ended up on the third floor usually didn't come out the same way they came in. It pleased him to be there since it was a lot more peaceful than the rest of the hospital.

There was an observation room next to Dr. Tom Black's office, where David would watch to make sure everything was going as planned. He would make sure that the nurse would not only forget what happened to her yesterday, but she would under go hypnosis. She would remember a different story now. The nurse also would be *one* of the first few city employees to try the new serum that the medical staff had been testing on specs.

David opened the door and found that he was the only one in the observational room. Some times there would be standing room only to watch the art of hypnotism with the magician, Dr. Black. Although, this wasn't exactly a planned and advertised training exercise. This had the same making of a secret spec trial, but only this time with a city employee.

David sat in a seat in the back corner of the empty room. A viewing place he preferred to any of the other options in the room. He sat in this same seat many times to watch med students observe a procedure. He crossed his legs and placed his hands over his right knee. He watched intently as the mayor's brother performed his magic.

Once again, a flawless hypnotic procedure was performed on the nurse. He often wondered why Tom limited his talents to Copperline. He could've easily been the highest in demand hypnotist in the world if he wanted to, and that's if he wasn't already.

Tom and David were often in this situation. David would administer whichever drug or serum needed, and Tom performed the process of guiding the patient back to the truth they needed them to believe. All of the spec guard trainees had been through similar process. After several years of testing on the specs, they felt that they had perfected the solution that would begin to strip residents of their memories. The serum would specifically alter cells in the hippocampus which would clear memories of their context. This would make it easier for Martin Black to control his people.

Tom, a lot like his older brother, was intent on keeping Copperline perfect. The order was their first priority. When Martin and Tom were young children, they would design plans and new constitutions that they would employ on the city once they were in charge. Tom never once questioned his older brother, but with faithfulness and dedication he always backed Martin up. It was a promise to his dying mother that he would support Martin in the best and worst of times.

David knew that Tom had loved his mother so much that he would comply to his mother's wishes, even though he wouldn't always approve of Martin's rash behavior or hunger for power.

Martin repeatedly pushed that David and Tom have the same passion and devotion for Copperline as himself. He had made it clear to them that he wouldn't be betrayed.

David watched as Tom finished up. *Amazing*, he thought to himself. *She'll think it was nothing more than a routine mental health check by the time he's done with her.* David smiled and shook his head. He got up from his seat and walked over to the glass.

David had the sound off, but he could see the nurse waking up. Tom stood and allowed time for the patient to stand. He had the woman do some routine stretches and movements to check her motor skills. He always had the patient engage in some breathing techniques as well. She was apparently passing with flying colors, as David noticed Tom holding out his hand for her to shake. She returned the offering and placed her other hand on top of the joined hands.

Tom opened the door for the nurse. She started through with a relaxed look on her face. David watched from the other side of the glass and turned on the volume. He watched as the nurse stopped in her tracks and turned around and faced Tom. Tom stood, unsure of why the woman stopped.

"You are something, Dr." The nurse smiled and reached out to touch his forearm. "Simply amazing." She leaned in and kissed him on the cheek before turning again to leave.

The action took Tom by surprise. Tom stood there for a moment as the nurse made her way down the hall. David chuckled and hit the intercom button from his side of the wall.

"Simply amazing, Doctor," David said with a laugh trailing his voice.

Tom looked at the glass and shook his head. His face was immediately cherry red with embarrassment. David shut the sound off to the intercom and came around through the door into Tom's office.

"I don't know how much you saw, but I can assure you that there were no inappropriate actions taken by me."

"You and your brother," David said shaking his head with a smile. "You have this whole city wrapped around your finger. Women love you, and men envy you."

Tom spoke up as he shut the door behind David. "What that woman did was inappropriate and should be grounds for punishment."

"Don't pretend like you don't like it, Tom. She's not married. You're not married. Just relax." David sat down on the same couch where the woman was sitting. "You can have any woman you want. Doesn't that ever entice you?"

"I have all that I want." Tom lifted his arms and motioned out the window which looked into downtown. "Sweet Copperline. She is the only one worthy of my attention. Men like us, David, simply don't have time for women. For love? Love is an illusion and intimacy is too messy."

"Ok, Dr. Phil…" David said still chucking.

"My brother's only fault was taking that wife and having those children." Tom crossed his arms, still looking out the window. "He's too distracted these days."

David, who was reclining, quickly set up. "Speaking of the devil." He tilted his head. "Yesterday was an interesting day. Did you hear?"

"My brother filled me in, yes." Tom moved away from the window to take a seat behind his desk.

"Well…" David said

"Well, what?" Tom asked.

"Well, *Tom*. This spec is showing very similar signs and tendencies as…"

"I get it." Tom interrupted the doctor. He sighed. "I understand."

"Can the world's best psych doctor reach inside that mind while the spec is unconscious and figure out what's happening inside there?" David pulled out his notepad from his pocket. "At times it's exhibited increased levels of pH balance, and because of that, it's exhibited supernatural bouts of strength." David became very animated with his hand gestures as he spoke.

Tom sat silently and listened.

"It's also apparently emitted enough radiation or electricity to blow up a containment room and crack the three-inch ballistic glass. When it's unconscious, it often talks to itself in languages that I've never come in contact with. One of the nurses thought it sounded Aramaic."

Tom lifted his hand to his chin. He could sense the warmth of his breath on the back of his hand as he exhaled through his nose.

"Martin said that Officer X128 found him by the tree?" Tom asked.

"That is correct," David said as he put the notebook back into his lab coat pocket.

"Sounds to me," Tom paused. "The officer may need the truth serum, and maybe a psych session. Maybe he holds a key to what happened to the spec. Maybe the truth is being suppressed?" Tom pulled out a binder from a bookshelf next to his desk. Separated by vocation, Tom flipped the security binder to the guards. "Sorry, what was the officer's ID number?"

"They call him Gerald, but his officer number is X128. A spec-raised, former trainee." David said without any hesitation.

"Gerald?" Tom squinted. "Why would they give a spec officer a name?"

"Beats me, Tom. The specs all call him X." David said as he stood and looked out the window to view Main Street.

"Right here. X128. He's Young. Really young. Not even 19? Doesn't list his donor names." Tom's finger scrolled over the information and tapped on the laminated piece of paper in the binder. "Yes. I'd say we bring him in. I'm going to call that brother of mine to see where this 'Gerald' got his name."

— C —

The phone rang. Martin's eyes shot open. A deep fogginess had overtaken him as he slowly woke up on the dining room floor where he had fallen asleep the night before. He never did hear Sarah come back down from the attic last night.

Where is that woman?

Martin walked over to the phone and looked at the caller ID as he answered. "Tom?"

"Good morning, Martin. I tried your office extension, but Maria said you hadn't come in yet. Is everything well, brother dear?" Tom said sarcastically.

"Everything is fine." Martin paced while holding the receiver to his ear. "Sarah and I are doing some remodeling, so I'm taking the morning off to meet with Henry. I'll be in the office soon."

"I see." Tom cleared his throat. "I just finished up with that nurse. She's cleared and is most likely returned to her home by now. Everything went as planned."

"Fantastic news. I knew I could count on you." Martin looked up the steps, but still no sign of either children or Sarah. *Where are they?*

"There's something more though." Tom paused. "I really think that we should interview this Officer X128."

"Tom, I really don't think that's necessary. He witnessed the medic's passing and detained the spec. What else do we need to know?"

"But he also witnessed the spec going into the tree and surviving." Tom made a valid point, but Martin had his mind made up on the matter.

"Look, Tom. I have this one taken care of." Martin snapped back. "Sorry, brother. I-"

"What's going on here, and why is David telling me that people are calling him Gerald?" Tom waited for his brother's punchy response, but the Mayor went silent. "Martin? Your silence is not very comforting."

"Tom." Martin was pulling for a response in his cluttered head. He drew his attention to the stairs again. He was still confused as to why his house was so still. Martin lifted his hand to rub his forehead. "Just trust me on this one. We may have bigger problems than X128."

"Martin?" Tom lifted his voice. "I've trusted you all my life and I've been your most diligent council member, but I'm worried. There is something else at stake here, isn't there?"

"Just stop it, Tom! I need you to just listen to me and not remind me of what kind of outstanding council member you *think* you are." Martin took a deep breath, and brought the phone closer to him as he lowered his voice. "Listen. I'm pretty certain that Mark, the medic who passed yesterday was writing down government secrets in a book. Right now, that book is nowhere to be found in the city. I had his locker cleaned, but it wasn't in there. When I brought the contents of the locker to the widow's house, I didn't see it there."

"What book?" Tom asked.

"*Art of War*, but that may not be the biggest problem." Martin grabbed the piece of paper from his pocket and studied it. "I think he has been writing very invasive and dangerous notes against us inside this book. For his wife, children, the specs? I don't know."

Tom closed his eyes and sighed. "What do we do, Martin?"

"We've got to find that book and see what he wrote in there. Despite the notes, it's still an unapproved book, and I don't want citizens to read books like that." Martin paused. "I especially don't want this copy to get into the wrong hands. I think it may be in the widow's house."

"Have you asked her," Tom asked.

"I started to hint around, but I never did come right out and ask. It was last night, during the Evening of Passing, and I may have pushed some of her buttons. I don't feel that she exactly has kosher feelings toward me anyway. The way she looks at me…"

"Forget how she looks at you. Focus! It's got to be here somewhere." Tom snapped.

Martin cleared his throat as he again looked up the stairs. "Have you and David ever thought about making an airborne option for the newest serum. If it worked so well for the nurse, I imagine it would work just fine on the widow."

Tom cursed. "Martin, we can't just bomb the city with agent orange. That's much too risky. You're talking about a drug that attacks the central nervous system and could have lasting negative reactions on different people. That's why we're starting with the specs. Only those that meet our criteria will experience it first."

"Risky or not, I would like the alchemists to began working on an airborne variation. Test it with the specs first." Tom realized as he heard his brother speak, it simply wouldn't matter what he thought. Martin always got what he wanted anyway. If Tom wouldn't convince the alchemists to begin the pursuit of an airborne strain, Martin would be there demanding them and threatening their livelihood.

"I'll have them get on it, but for now we need a different way to get to the widow," Tom said. "What about the son? I surely know that young public policy students are really eager to get an early intro to the program. Is there any value in getting the son in now, and trying the serum on him first?"

"*Now*, brother of mine. That's aligning yourself to the mayor's mind." Martin's voice was sarcastic as he knew that Tom would be rolling his eyes.

"I'll set that up. He'll buckle. He's eager to join the program, and he'll be my guest tonight for dinner. We'll give him the truth serum soon, and see if he qualifies for the new serum as well," Martin said.

Tom took out his file for Mark Waters Jr. and was already looking at his medical records. "Blood type A positive. In great health. Normal blood pressure. Actually, blood pressure looks a little lower than others his age. That's a plus. He's young and has a good GPA, which means he has good blood flow to the brain. It says he that he runs every day? Good motor skills then too. It looks like he mostly qualifies already. We just have to see how he does while on the truth serum."

Martin listened and smiled.

"In fact, I'll set up a meeting with Mark's counselor today at the high school and get the ball rolling on his early introduction to politics," Tom said.

Martin was smiling as he heard his brother tell him exactly everything he wanted to hear. He loved it when that happened. Martin would've done it anyway, but it's nice to have unity. Rarely was Martin swayed by his council members, but it was pleasant to hear his brother saying such favorable things.

It had always been unfortunate for a council member to disagree with Martin. Usually, there followed a series of unfortunate events that led to the disobedient council member's removal from their council seat, and at times even removal from Copperline.

Martin spoke quietly, but confidently into the receiver. "By the time we're done with him, we'll have Mark Waters Jr. squealing like a dirty little swine."

Nine

Sara had slept in the attic. She awoke to the sound of Martin's shoe slamming into the floorboards next to her head. The loud sound woke the two children. He watched as his wife's eyes opened wide in confusion and pain. Each of them looked back to behold the tall man with dark features looking down at them with a contemptuous grin.

Martin looked at the children with duct tape over their mouths and hands and feet bound by rope. He looked at Sarah who was sitting down in a fetal position with her arms around her knees. He could see that her makeup was streaked by tears. He was irritated that she was intentionally avoiding eye contact with him, as she often did when she was upset at him.

"You've been crying a lot lately, dear." *Probably when she was binding the children*, he thought. "You're growing soft in your old age, Sarah." He looked at her and shook his head.

"What do we do, Martin?" Her shaky voice spoke, but she wouldn't look at him.

"I've had this under control for all these years. I'll figure this out now." He looked at his wife with a deep anger because of her blatant disapproval of him. He kept control of his voice and his temper. "I hate that you doubt me so much, Sarah. I hate how you disrespect me in front of our children."

"Martin, please. Can we not do this in front of the children?" She spoke through tears. She looked at the children who were looking back at their mother.

"Stand up." Martin demand.

"Martin, please." She shook her head as she finally looked at Martin. Her eyes begged him not to do anything, but like so many previous times in her married life, he paid no attention to that.

Martin took two steps toward her and grabbed her by the arm. The twins protested beneath their duct tape. The girl had tears streaming down her face. Martin watched the girl's tears rolls off the tape that was covering her mouth as she clenched her eyes shut tight. He had no remorse. He was too angered by Sarah to feel anything else. The boy started shaking his head and moaning continuously, but the mayor looked at his wife's fearful expression.

Martin brought Sarah to himself and held her there tightly. "When I say stand up," he paused. His voice went from a passive-aggressive tone to a piercing scream. "I mean stand up!"

The children were both crying now as Martin threw his wife down on the attic floor. Walking over to her limp body, he spat in her face.

He gained composure again and settled his temper down. "Get yourself up, and pull yourself together. Get yourself in order before Henry gets here." He wiped the spittle from his lips. "I'll expect you on your best behavior, yes?"

Sarah started crying aloud on the floor. She turned her face away from the children.

"It's no use, Sarah. Turn your head all you want! You're weak. You're soft, and they can see it now." He moved toward the attic door. "Hurry up, and get downstairs so you can tend to your other children."

— C —

Martin headed down the stairs. Sarah slowly made her way back up off the floor. She wiped the tears from her face and embraced her two children who were trying to suppress their cries. She took the little girl's face in her hands and held her forehead against her's. "Mommy loves you two so much." She held the boy close to her. "I'm going to fix this, I promise you."

The children looked at her and nodded gently.

— C —

As Martin got to the bottom of the stairs he noticed Margret's dark hair and big brown eyes peeking out through her door. He made it obvious to her that he knew she was there, but he said nothing. He knew that she was wondering what the noises were from upstairs. Her eyes watched every step he made.

Entering the kitchen, Martin reached for the receiver, but he noticed Bradley again standing in the dining room.

"Bradley? Son, what are you doing?" Bradley stood motionless. Martin shook Bradley's shoulder. "Son!"

Bradley turned to face his father. As he turned, Martin could see that he had been crying.

"Son. Not you too! Fix yourself up." Martin shook his head in disapproval. "Gentlemen never cry."

"Sorry, Father." Bradley finally whimpered in a soft voice. He looked at the newly boarded up section in the wall.

"Get yourself together, son. I am getting Henry over here today to fix this mess." Martin pointed at the fireplace.

"Why did you cover up the fireplace?" Bradley asked as he brushed the tears from his eyes. "Who is he, Father?"

"Son, go to your room and pull yourself together now." Martin pointed to the stairs.

Bradley started walking up the stairs as he noticed Sarah making her way down holding Margret's hand.

Paying no attention to them, he continued to the phone and dialed Henry's number.

"Good morning, Mayor!" Henry always answered Martin's calls.

"Good morning, Henry. My wife and I are expecting company tonight, but there are some urgent projects that we need to make sure are fixed before dinner tonight." Martin watched his wife and daughter from the next room.

Sarah started braiding and brushing Margret's hair. Martin still had a sense of anger possessing him, but the sight made him pause and feel a very confusing emotion. He knew it wasn't love, because his great leader would never allow it. It was more like…

"Mayor, you know I can't say no to you." Henry sounded like he was going through. "Let me just see what I can move around here, and I'll be over as soon as I can. Does that work?"

"Yes. Henry, I can't thank you enough!" Martin kicked a table leg to get his wife's attention. Sarah turned her head toward him without making eye contact. She nodded at the sound of the plan being established. "I will be at my office, and my wife is taking the children to the market. Do you still have the temporary code from last time?"

"Yes, sir."

Henry handled each remodel to the Hurd Manor. He had been trusted by Martin very much. Ever since he was a child, and

Martin's grandfather needed a remodel at the manor. Henry was a lot younger then, but out of the handful of carpenters in the city, Henry was the most reliable. He also honored Martin's wish to not reveal anything he had seen inside the mayor's manor.

"Great. Thanks again, Henry." Martin sighed. This would buy him time to go to the lab and check on the spec and perhaps have conversations with David and Tom.

David had been getting on Martin's nerves as of late. He was irritated that so much seemed to go wrong while on the doctor's watch. He and David have always had a successful partnership, but Martin knew that all men could be replaced if need be. Past victories or not, Martin would not be made a fool. He would not tolerate incompetence. Henry, in Martin's eyes, was always faithful to the city and didn't have an incompetent bone in his body.

— C —

Sarah sat and started to listen to the phone conversation. Martin kicked the table to get her attention. She watched him mouth the words, "dinner" to her. She felt a pain in the pit of her stomach. *The dinner.* She had dreaded dinner. With everything that had been going on in the past few days, her mind was a mess.

Dinner was the last thing she wanted to do this evening. She began to resent that man more and more. Copperline seemed to be the perfect lover that Sarah could never be. There was never any doubt that Martin didn't love her, but he was only using the people around him to control. While he made it appear to citizens that they were in love, there were too many secrets hidden well within the Hurd Manor.

It was always an agonizing task, putting on the plastic smile and pretending like her life was so perfect. Sarah hated her life,

Copperline, and every time Martin would hit her. It became a daily ritual of applying makeup to cover up bruises. *All the sacrifices I make,* she thought. *And Martin comes home smelling like a perfume that's not mine.*

Most of all, Sarah hated that she had nobody to share her feelings with. She was alone in the city of plastic people. Forced to keep to herself for 22 years of their marriage, resentment crept into her heart.

Thoughts of her dinner guest tonight toyed with her. In a way, she envied Mellissa. Sarah had many times wished for herself to become a widow. From dreams of her and her four children leaving to escaping through the gates of Copperline and running until shelter was found. She had no knowledge of what was beyond the city limits, but she didn't care.

There was an undying love and compassion for her children and she would willingly sacrifice her life. All four of them were so incredibly unique, yet all an impression of her. It was a relief to her that not one of them resembled Martin's dark ways. How a man that evil could create such pure-hearted children was a mystery.

Sarah had no idea how they would explain the attic children to the city as they got older. Martin would always come up with something that the city would believe.

"Mother?"

Startled by the tiny voice, Sarah found herself sitting with her head tilted daydreaming with the brush still in Margret's hair.

Margret turned her tiny head and looked into her mother's eyes. She whispered, "are you okay, momma?"

Sarah smiled and nodded as a single tear fell from her eye. She leaned in and kissed Margret on the cheek. "You're so beautiful," she whispered in her daughter's ear. She held her in that position for a moment. Sarah may have needed that embrace even more than Margret, who had been sniffling little tiny tears as well. "I love you," Sarah whispered.

Margret smiled and replied, "more than a lot."

She loved hearing about how Bradley wanted to be an architect and build great structures that stand the test of time. He would often ask to research different bridges and skyscrapers throughout the world. Even though his findings were always limited by what they were allowed to have in the school system, he was always fascinated by building techniques and how engineers were always asking how to make things better.

She often thought of all the mothers that had given birth to all of those specs that were held in the basement of the hospital. She pitied them for not even knowing that they had other children. Some were mothers of twins, and some were mothers of what they thought were stillbirths. In secret, the doctors determined what they would do midway through the mother's pregnancy. She pitied herself for knowing too much.

She wondered whose child the spec was that they were holding in containment. She sighed to herself. She wasn't allowed to know who the donors were, which made it easier seeing people around the city. Though, she could always assume when a woman had a still birth, that she unknowingly just donated a spec.

She kept brushing Margret's hair while Martin got himself ready to head into the office. This was therapy for her. Though watching him get ready was not like it was 22 years ago. It used to be something that she loved so much, but soon into their marriage, he changed. He may have promised her love and kindness, but instead he was filled with lust and anger. He pressured her and made her feel uncomfortable in ways that only left her shameful.

She noticed that he was wearing his gray suit, which usually meant he was preparing to make a statement on CTV. Which must've meant he was preparing for something to go wrong.

She hated that he could talk his way out of anything. She was convinced that he could murder her, and play it off as some kind of accident. He would have the entire city wrapped around his finger even more. He could have a bedroom full of harlots and none of the residents would even bat an eyelash because it was the perfect, Martin Black. *Who could resist him?* She said to herself sarcastically.

She continued to brush Margret's hair, but the brush slipped from her hand and fell to the floor. As she went to grab the brush, she noticed a number of floorboards spreading and popping up.

She tilted her head and watched as a couple boards made a loud snapping noise as they quickly sprang out of place. The room filled with the unbearable scent of sulfur again.

"Mother, the smell," Margret whispered as she pointed to the boards. "It's coming from the basement?"

Martin was putting on cufflinks in the other room when he heard the floor snapping. He stepped around the corner and raised his nose to the air in such a way that let Sarah know he could also smell the offensive stench rising from the basement.

Sarah watched as Martin sighed, walked to the basement door and tried to pull it open, but it wouldn't budge. He cursed out loud.

"It's good thing Henry is coming right over." Sarah stood and watched Martin's unsuccessful attempt to pull the door open.

Martin looked up at his wife and glared at her as he straightened his sleeves that he rolled up in his attempt to open the door. He said not a word, but only stared with no emotion.

"I'll be back later this evening before dinner." Martin adjusted his suit jacket over his shirt. "Please have this house looking like a home." He looked at himself in the living room mirror while he straightened his tie.

Sarah hung her head. She felt defeated again. He had an incredible ability to perpetually take the wind from her sails.

"Now, come give your husband a kiss." Martin pointed to his cheek.

Sarah slowly made her way over to Martin. She picked her head up as if she was going to kiss him on the lips, but turned her head at the last second and whispered into his ear, "don't count on it."

Martin couldn't help but grin, and she hated that he did. *Did that amuse you?* She thought.

"You know," Martin started to say in a whisper as he straightened the sleeves of this shirt under the jacket. "Maria has always been quite fond of this suit."

Her face immediately turned into a scowl. She felt heat from her core rise up in her as she was angered by his remark. Humiliated by his hubris, her eyes instantly roamed the area for a knife or some kind of blade she could stab him with, but there was nothing. Not that she would ever do anything like that in front of the children, but she wanted to threaten him. She wanted know what it felt like to hold the power.

"Well then Maria's a…"

Her words were cut short as she felt a tight grip around her neck. She looked at her husband as an invisible force lifted her feet from the ground. Sarah was now eye level to the tall man. She grasped at her neck and started to choke.

"Mm," she tried to speak as tears fell down her face. "Mar…" She tried to look and see if the child were watching. In her efforts to speak and breathe, she coughed. She could see that he was still fixing his clothing, but she felt the sensation of fingers closing her airways. The grip grew tighter and tighter around her neck. She knew her face must've been turning purple.

"Sorry, my dear. Were going to say something?" Martin asked with a slight grin as he leaned in to his wife's ear. He whispered, "you really should see how lucky you are. Do you know how many women envy you?"

Martin kissed her softly on the cheek as she felt the invisible grip around her neck release and her body fell hard to the floor. She coughed and started wheezing for air. Her hands rubbed her neck.

Martin moved past her and made his way toward the children. He kissed them each on the forehead and said in a boisterous tone, "Bradley, keep an eye on these two today. You're in charge son. Show me that you can handle the responsibility of being mayor. Don't let a woman dictate how you lead."

"Of course, Father." Bradley stood there delighted at his father's trust in him. He had envisioned himself as the future mayor of Copperline ever since he knew of his father's vocation.

Sarah sat there on the floor still frozen and completely disgusted by her husband's remarks. She wouldn't look, but only listened to the sound of him leaving.

She couldn't help but feel a little sense of liberty every time he walked out the door. It became her drug of choice, and she wanted more of it. She could focus when he wasn't always demanding. She could breathe easier without him there. She would now be able to think about what she had to do later that night.

— C —

Martin walked to his cart and slipped into the seat. He would undoubtedly meet people at the gate that would be wondering why he didn't go into the office during his normal time, but he was ready. He was always ready.

In his mind, it was aggravating that people continually asked questions about every little detail about his life, but he was attempting to create the perfect society. A little white lie was completely harmless if it meant people felt safe. However, sometimes Martin wondered which lies carried more numeric value, mathematically of course.

If lying to Sarah about working late at the Citadel was valued at a ten, how much would a story that covered up a spec escaping a secret government facility be worth? Or what about coving up the fact that the beloved mayor had two secret children he kept in his attic?

He often wondered if Tom had these thoughts as well.

Martin drove his cart to the gate of the Hurd Manor where it opened slowly for him. As expected, a few people were standing by waiting to speak to him.

"Mayor Black, good morning!"

"Good morning, neighbor!" Martin nodded and waved. "How do you find yourself on this beautiful day?"

"I'm well, thank you." The man smiled. "Getting a mid-morning start today? Is everything okay, Mayor?"

"Yes! My wife and I are finally refinishing the original floors in the manor and we were prepping everything for the carpenters." Martin explained.

"Excellent! Have a great day, Mayor." The man nodded in approval and held out his hand for the mayor to shake. A few more did as well.

The mayor smiled and shook the hands of the men in the crowd. As each man approached his cart, he watched as the each smiled and nodded. He also returned the nod.

"You all have an incredible day! To neighbors!" He shouted and waved as he started to accelerate through the crowd.

"To neighbors!" They cheered. Some clapped, and the others waved.

Martin was off to the Citadel.

The citadel was Martin's favorite place to be. It's where he felt most important. He felt power from his mayoral position. He felt control, but yearned for even more. He would spend a lot of his time with the alchemists. He felt that they were so close to something groundbreaking. It was something that he would take with him when he would eventually expand his political horizons.

From mayor to the senate, then finally to the white house. To a new world order that would give me complete control, he imagined to himself as he drove his cart through the city. He travelled the same roads every day and delighted in the downtown skyline as he approached it.

Just ahead of him, Martin could see the white-domed roof of the citadel. He felt his mobile phone vibrating in his jacket pocket.

He would normally avoid it, but the last couple of days gave him reason for him to answer it. He pulled off the side of the road but made sure that nobody was watching him. Only few people in Copperline had access mobile phones, he never wanted to draw attention to it.

It was David.

"What's wrong?" Martin answered.

"Taking a vacation day?" David and his sarcastic tone was no match for Martin's thin patience.

"I'm on my way now," Martin said.

"Meet me in the subway." David ended the call immediately.

Martin sighed out of his nostrils and continued on his way.

— C —

Upon arriving at the Citadel, Martin entered the main foyer and into the lobby of the city council. Just one stop at his office, then to the subway. His objective was to avoid all small talk since he was starting the day so late.

The door to his office was just ahead of him. Maria waited outside his door at her desk with a pile of folders and paperwork.

"Mayor Black! I have this for you, but also you have messages from the maintenance crew who went outside the East Gate to check on the propane silo. They left their credentials inside and they can't get back in." Maria spoke as he approached her desk.

"Ok, Maria. I'll call someone from security and have them head down and deal with it." Martin fumbled for his office key and badge.

"Yes, sir." Maria smiled. "Would you like me to call?"

"I'll call, Maria! Please, just…" He exhaled and calmed himself down. "I'm sorry for that. Thank you for informing me." Martin unlocked his door with his badge and quickly walked in.

In the office, he set the pile of paperwork down on his desk and began searching for another key. Martin found the key that unlocked the only drawer with a lock. He slid it open and reached his hand inside.

Pausing to see if anybody in the courtyard was looking in, he felt his hand touched the cold metal of the pistol. The feel of the metal against his fingers made him quiver for a second. He studied the object. He watched as he touched it as he ran them over the words, Ruger.

What are you doing, Martin? He tried to convince himself to leave it in it's place while he also tried to convince himself to pick it up.

A knock on the door startled him. He closed and locked the drawer.

"Come in." Martin grabbed the folder to make it look like he had been busy at work.

Maria stood at the door with Officer X128. "Sir, Officer X128 says he has an urgent matter to speak with you about."

"Yes, please do come in, X." Martin motioned to his chair in front of his desk. X made his way over to the chair while Maria shut the door behind her.

"What's going on, Gerald?" Martin's tone changed and his voice lowered.

"Some guys are getting antsy because your brother is asking a lot of questions." X rubbed his forehead with both hands. "I wasn't completely honest with you, alright?"

"Whatever happened, happened." Martin looked out his window. "Right now, I'm trying to save you from a truth serum trial. Hell, I'm trying to save myself from a truth serum trial."

"People are starting to ask why they heard you call me Gerald." He shook his head back. "What do I tell them?"

"That's easy. Tell them you reminded me of the saxophone player, Gerald Albright." Martin smiled.

"I don't know who that is, but is that really why?" X asked.

"You're mother and I loved his music at the time." Martin met his gaze. "Of course when she passed during your delivery, I wanted something to remember her by. It just seemed appropriate."

"Ok. Ok." X nodded. "I apologize for the inappropriate behavior. I'll pull myself together. I hear there are some boneheaded utility workers who are locked outside the east gate?"

"That's right. They need a proper city worker to remind them how we operate in Copperline." Martin smiled at X. "And Gerald. If things get haywire today, or tomorrow, or even next week, please know that I've never been more proud of anybody in this city."

X stood tall while trying to suppress a smile. "Thank you, Father."

Ten

David waited in the empty subway for over an hour. Patience was not a virtue that he had developed over his years. He paced back and forth, looking at his watch every few minutes. Irritated by Martin's tardiness, he pulled out his mobile device and dialed Tom.

"Black," Tom answered.

"Hold off. He's not here yet." David's voice was not the usual sarcastic tone, it was more rushed and anxious. "Do you still have X229 there?"

"Yes, David. Trust me. Trust us. This will all be back to normal by this evening." Tom tried to put David at ease. "We've been doing this for years."

"Yes, but your brother is harboring secrets from *us*." David couldn't suppress the anger in his voice.

"David, you need to calm down. If Martin suspects that you're all of a sudden out to get him, he'll make sure you're quickly silenced. Good alchemists can be trained here in Copperline."

"Is that a threat, Tom?" David snarled into the receiver.

"No, but it is a reality." Tom paused and let the line go quiet. He could hear the heavy breathing of his angered companion. "David. This will all be fine by this evening. Have you interviewed all the other medics and nurses to see if they found that book?"

"Yes. Nobody has seen it anywhere." David's voice calmed.

"Right now, that's our biggest concern. We can keep the other medic, and X229 quiet." Tom laughed. "You and I have enough drugs to create an airborne virus that could wipe everybody's memory out. We could have everybody programmed by the end of the week to make all of them think that you're the Dali Lama."

"I hear footsteps. I'm assuming Martin's." David looked down the subway hall. "Just postpone the psych treatment on X229 until Martin and I get there." David ended the call right then.

"David, is that you I hear?" Martin stepped into his line of sight.

"Martin. We are finding out certain things." David's voice began to get shaky. "Things that you're either keeping from us, or worse, they are being withheld from you, and we are being played. I don't like being played, Martin!"

"David, calm down." Martin rolled his eyes, "What things?"

"Tom and I interviewed the other officer and the medic that was there yesterday on the scene where Mark was killed." David began coughing like he was getting ready to dry heave. "Two of them were telling different stories so we gave them a truth serum trial. They spilled it, Martin. It was X128 who killed the medic, not the spec."

Martin's face turned red instantly and distorted, "You allowed *yourself* to do a truth serum trial without my consent? Why do you feel that you need to go behind my back? And why are you dry heaving?" Martin winced at David as he moved closer to him. "Don't you start getting weak on me too, Dr. Jacobs! I always thought you were better than this!"

"Martin, I-" David began backing up until his body slammed against the wall. His eyes widened with terror. He was being held against the hard surface by an invisible force as if he was magnetized to it.

"Do you remember the agreement that we all made?" Martin pounded his fingers into David's chest. "Don't you go back on your word, Doctor."

"Your brother…" David tried to speak, but his voice went suddenly mute.

David now felt a a burning sensation in his throat. He could see down the hall, past the tall frame of Martin, the yellow and orange fire that he once saw years ago.

Martin's voice thundered and echoed through the tunnel. Almost too loud for the doctor to bare. "Don't you worry about my brother and me, and don't you dare go back on your word, David!" He screamed into the doctor's ear.

David couldn't talk. His eyes frantically went from Martin, then to the approaching light. His nostrils were filled with the rancid smell of sulfur.

"Don't do it, David! Don't you do it!" Martin's eyes went completely black, reflecting the approaching fire. He grabbed David's neck. His large hands could almost wrap entirely around David's neck.

David, still unable to talk, violently shook his head and mouthed the words, 'no.'

Suddenly the fire subsided and Martin took his hand away from David. His face returned to an emotion-less expression. "That's good that we remember our agreements." Martin's voice was normal again. "Consider yourself to have been blessed to receive such a valuable lesson."

"Lesson?" David was rubbing his neck with his right hand. He looked at the Mayor, rubbing his hands.

"Humans learn best from trauma. Is that not so, Doctor?" Martin adjusted his gray blazer and the knot of his tie. "What are you worried about anyway, old man?"

"I just thought…"

Martin held up his hand, inches from his David's face. "That's your problem. You *think* too much. There's no need to try to unpack this labyrinthian mind that I possess."

"I'm sorry to have doubted you, Martin." David hung his head as he talked.

"Please. I feel that our relationship has become too personal. It's Mayor Black from now on, or at least until I feel that you have regained my trust." Martin held his stare awaiting David's reply.

"Yes, sir."

"The only thing I want you to be concerned about right now is that missing book. Find it and keep the spec quiet." Martin turned and walked back down the hallway from the same direction he came.

Martin could see in his mind, David rubbing his neck with a concerned look on his face.

He walked back through the tunnels shaking his head. *What do I have to do to get everybody on the same page as me?*

His frustrations grew as he thought about the situation. The order in this city was his first priority and *his* responsibility. He walked as he listened to his shoes against the surface of the floor. For whatever reason unknown to him, the clacking sound that it made against the hard stone put his at ease.

Approaching the door that led to the courtyard, he swiped his card and waited for the green light. Martin entered the familiar sight of the stone walkways, open ceiling, and elaborate fountains in the center of the citadel courtyard. He walked through without stopping and entered into the office lobby where he found Maria working at her desk, just in front of his door.

"Mayor." Maria winked at him.

Martin was straight-faced. He cursed under his breath. "Not today, Maria."

"Sir." Maria looked away as he entered his office.

He walked into his office, closed the door and went directly to his desk. He reached in a side drawer and pulled out a small laptop. Martin opened an application of the city's surveillance system. The Mayor pulled up a few houses in the East End, studying the houses from many different angles.

He assumed they all should be empty, except for the house of an old widow who had been on bed rest for some time. “Mrs. Roy, you won’t be too much trouble now, will you?”

Flipping through the many of the camera feeds, he convinced himself that he had to move now. He would not be overtaken by a book. His mission was to find and destroy that book.

— C —

Tom was in his office when he received a call from Martin.

“Black,” Tom answered.

“Tom, *what* is going on?” Martin asked his brother.

“I was wondering that myself. We have a forced confession from two witnesses stating that X is the murderer. We have paperwork here from 19 years ago that was from X’s anonymous donors with a lot of your signatures everywhere. I don’t see many other delivery contracts with your signatures except for four others. Two from Bradley and Margret, but then two more.” Tom waited to hear what kind of story Martin would come up with now.

Martin sighed. “They’re all mine. All five.”

Tom went silent.

“Gerald’s mother passed in the delivery. Sarah and I thought it’d be best if he went into the guard training program.” Martin’s voice was completely emotionless and hushed.

Silence remained in the air. Tom could feel his jaw clenching tight. He could sense his stomach becoming as if he was going to be sick.

“Tom…”

“Martin, how am I supposed to process this news? Here is something that you have been keeping from me for 19 years, and now we’ve got other potential problems to contend with.”

"Tom, I'm counting on you to pull yourself together and look past this." Martin was quick to answer. "Don't get soft on me, Tom. Just like Sarah. Just like David."

While he expected his brother to lash out at him, Martin's voice was low and somewhat composed. *What are you up to, brother?*

"Sarah?" Tom questioned. "I never agreed with your marriage because it's completely a sham, but why are you bringing her into this? What have you done?"

While his voice was still hushed, his demeanor changed. "She is growing soft, Thomas! Don't you get soft on me too. We made an agreement! We made an oath to preserve Copperline!"

"Martin, stop!" Tom pulled up the surveillance application on his mobile tablet. "Where are you? You're not in your office, but the call came in as your office line."

Martin sighed. "Tom put your computer away and stop searching for me like some pathetic school girl wondering where her lover is."

Tom pulled up all the areas where Martin would frequently visit, but there was no sign of him anywhere. "Why don't we meet in the subway. We can talk more freely."

"I can't Tom. I've got an appointment. Make the announcement to the school that we are accepting the applicants early. Get started on that now." Martin ended the call on his mobile phone.

Tom knew that his brother must've been well hidden at the moment and this made him very uneasy. "What are you doing, Martin?" Tom said quietly.

— C —

Mark Jr. listened to the sound of the lunch bell. He found himself wondering how his sister was doing, but he especially worried about his mother.

He picked up his books from his desk and joined the rest of his class who were leaving the room in a neat and orderly fashion.

Mark Jr. opened his locker and placed his books amongst the others. He liked to read fiction while he was on lunch. While some of his peers preferred company on their breaks, his ideal time away from class included getting lost in one of the great classics.

He grabbed his novel, but as he did another book the fell to the ground. He bent down to get the fallen object, *The Art of War*. He quickly grabbed it and returned it to the locker. He knew that he meant to bring that book home because it was on the unauthorized book list. He looked around as nonchalantly as possible to see if anyone else had noticed. To his relief, it appeared that nobody was paying any attention.

"I need you to read everything in this book, Son. Pay no attention to the fact that it's not allowed. If anything, it's for that very reason you need to read it." He remembered his father telling him just days before he passed. Mark Sr. surprised his son for lunch that day at the school. "I also have added many notes of my own in the back that your mother will need to see as well. Guard it, Son."

Mark Jr. intended on reading it after he finished his current book, but he couldn't believe that he left it in his locker. Getting caught with that would be grounds for immediate expulsion and maybe even removal from Copperline. "Don't be stupid, Mark." He shook his head as he spoke to himself.

Mark shut his locker and headed to lunch and promised himself he would bring that book home after school this afternoon.

He also brought with him a legal pad to write down questions and speaking points for the mayor later at dinner. Mark had long awaited for a chance to speak to the mayor. He would've preferred a better circumstance to do so, but it made his father's passing a lot easier to handle.

While he knew his mother didn't necessarily care too much to dine with the Black family, he and his sister would love the opportunity to learn more about city government. It was a world that Mark felt a strong connection and a need to be a part of. He wanted to become a city council member in the worst way.

Making his way outside of the building, he decided to eat his lunch on the grass today, isolated from as many of his peers as possible. He knew that to be a council member, he should probably be making connections and networking even at a young age, but the introvert in him called most of the shots.

The warm California sun was more than a delight as he felt it shining on his face. He found a vine maple tree to sit against and took advantage of its shade, Mark opened the book and started to lose himself within the words once again.

— C —

Mellissa had dropped all of her late husband's belongings at the transfer container as instructed. She had almost missed the deadline, but resolved that she would just hide the rest of the contents in her basement.

Thinking of what an asinine policy it was, to dispose of the belongings from a passed loved one. Sarah convinced herself that others must hold on to more than their allotted amount of heirlooms. She had a lot that she wanted to hold on to. She was connected to Mark with a love that the grave couldn't break apart.

She walked away from the large metal container with tears in her eyes. She was careful to keep her head down since it was beyond her allowed mourning time and she was in public. Tears would surely get her in trouble with city officials.

Looking over to her right, she heard people talking by the East Gate. She never cared for this area of the city, mainly because it was so bland. The West Gate was beautiful and people marveled at. The expansion happened so fast in the East End, that the decor didn't receive as much attention as the other places in Copperline.

One of the officers started raising his voice to men in utility uniforms. "If you do this again, you'll be subpoenaed to appear before the council and have to get reinstated as residents."

She listened while she kept her distance. The last thing she wanted was to be seen by anyone in her condition. It didn't take much to get subpoenaed in Copperline, so she pitied the workers that were getting yelled at.

She walked faster to return back to her cart, but it wasn't fast enough.

"Ma'am please stop and show your ID." She heard the officer call out.

Mellissa brought her forearm to her face to wipe away and tears. She sighed as she stopped and reached into her purse to find her ID card.

"Ma'am, I'm sorry. You can move along." The officer softened his tone as he approached her. "I didn't recognize you at first. I know we are not supposed to talk like this, but I'm so sorry for your loss."

She offered a polite smile with tears forming in her eyes again. She held out her hand to shake his. "Thank you, Officer. That's very kind of you."

He held out his hand in return and shook hers. "Please, everybody calls me X."

Her hand froze in his. A cold rush of blood filled her head. She recognized him as the one who gave the report of Mark's death on

CTV. She had hundreds of questions, but she knew she wasn't allowed to ask.

"X." Was the only thing she managed to speak. She slowly nodded.

"Yes, ma'am. Again, I'm so sorry." He offered his sympathy again.

Why was he so apologetic? People at the celebration of life weren't even this sympathetic. She thought to herself.

She pulled her hand back and tried to keep it together. "Did you work with my husband much?"

"Yes, ma'am. We were usually assigned to the same downtown sector." He let his arms hang to his side. "Medics and guards work together a lot, especially in the downtown sector."

"I see." She said as she fixed the strap of her purse over her shoulder. She almost thought she could see his eyes getting cloudy. "I'm sorry to distract you from your duties." She said as she directed her attention to the maintenance men still waiting to finish getting yelled at.

"Right." He said as he followed her gaze. "Just some utility workers. Nothing to be concerned about."

"I understand. I'm not concerned or worried." She smiled. Though inside, she remembered the letter from the spec to her husband that talked about this man. "You saw Mark when he passed?"

"I'm sorry ma'am." He interrupted her. "I'm not at liberty to talk about details."

Her heart sank again. Knowing that he wouldn't say anything. "I understand."

"Have a good day, ma'am," X said with a gentle smile.

"Sir." She said and watched him turn and begin to readdress the maintenance workers in a tone that seemingly mimicked compassion.

Mellissa hung her head again and continued her path back to her cart.

— C —

Martin slowly made his way through the unfamiliar territory. He only knew a little about this house from the few times monitoring surveillance prior to his arrival. He quietly made is way up the stairs from the basement, where he snuck into the Waters' house. He kept watching his mobile device which was set to a camera of Mellissa's driveway.

Making his way through the kitchen and living room, he was disgusted at the mess. He looked at boxes with loose papers strewn all over the table and counter. The sink was full of dishes and one of the cabinet doors was left open. He assumed it was pertinent to the recent passing of Mellissa's husband, but it sickened him. *What kind of people live like this?* He thought to himself as his eyes frantically searched for the book. Searching every shelf on the main floor of the house for words that read *The Art of War.*

"Where is it?" He whispered to himself.

No sign of the book.

Knowing it was pushing it now, he started toward the staircase that led upstairs. *Careful, she only went to the East Gate. She'll be home soon,* he heard a voice remind him in his head. He brought up the surveillance camera of the East Gate relieved to see that she was still there. He watched and zoomed in on Mellissa having a conversation with X128. He tilted his head at the sight. *What's happening there?*

He watched the screen as he brought each foot closer to the second floor, step after step. Martin's hand slid slowly over the handrail as he ascended. The mayor could smell a powder-like fragrance and found it more desirable than the main floor.

Taking his focus off the screen for a moment, he told himself to speed the process. The top stair caught his shoe by surprise and Martin found himself quickly falling to the carpeted floor. The device bounced and slid across the floor. Martin cursed and pounded the floor. He jumped to his feet swiftly and reached for the device. It slammed into his hand from across the hallway like his hand was a magnet. He checked the device, which was slightly cracked down the front of the screen. Brushing his pants and cracking his neck, he regained his posture and continued forward.

He started opening each bedroom door and tried to quickly search the contents of the room with his eyes, but nothing stuck out to him. He glanced back at the screen to see there was no longer an image of Mellissa and X talking together. The mayor saw that her cart was gone. Martin quickly swiped over to the surveillance feed of her driveway. She hadn't returned yet, but he had to assume she would be there soon.

He made his way back down the stairs. One hand sliding down the railing, and one hand holding the device. He checked the screen to see the image of her empty driveway.

Breathing heavily, Martin stood on the bottom step of the staircase. He looked at the first floor again and sighed. Disgusted and frustrated, he desired to make the home go up in flames, but the mayor restrained himself. *The book could be somewhere hidden inside.* He needed to know what was written in there. A strange attachment was being formed to it, almost as if it possessed a great power that made him powerless.

He made his way out of the living room and back into the kitchen. Suddenly, he heard the squeal from the breaks of Mellissa's cart. He hurried down the stairs to the rear bulkhead where he let himself in.

He slowly opened the doorknob that preceded the bulkhead. Opening the door quietly knowing that she would be entering the house in just a matter of seconds, the mayor looked at the surveillance application again. She was still in her cart with her head hanging down on the steering wheel.

Martin took advantage of the time and quickly pushed up the bulkhead door and slipped out. He knew to do this in mid daylight was a risky move, but he had the camera feeds of the houses in the area in the palm of his hand. He saw that most of their driveways were empty, other than Mrs. Roy, the older citizen on bedrest who was reading a book. Her bedroom window was on the opposite side of the house and didn't face the Waters' house.

Martin crept along the side of the house and through the gate that led him through neighbor's yard. Just one more yard and it would put him on the street.

This was almost too easy, he thought to himself making his way into the last neighbor's yard.

He kept with his back to the house as he crouched. As he crept, Martin could hear the sound of the crushed granite stone that was right up against the house's foundation.

Making his way back to the concrete road, he slipped his mobile device in his packet and started walking to his cart, which was parked just a few blocks up past the park.

A sudden sensation came over him that he was being watched. He stopped walking as he heard steps behind him. He thought the sound was coming from slippers or sandals. Martin slowly turned and looked back.

"Mayor Black? I believe you have some explaining to do."

Eleven

I stood in the stillness. A blueish-white all around me. I found myself slipping into a dream-like realm quite often, which meant I was most likely in a comatose state again. *Why haven't they killed me yet?*

They, inevitably wanted answers. For whatever reason, they needed to know what happened in that tree. Which told me, that it had to be a reoccurring problem.

Why are specs running to that tree? Am I the only one that got out? What are the sarcophagi they are being held in? I started thinking of those bodies on the cave ceiling with the roots wrapped them. I shivered at the thought. I was still trying to make sense of all this, myself. I felt inadequate to answer any questions at all. I remembered the voices saying that I was called there. *But why?*

I couldn't see or feel any part of my body right at that point.

Then I thought of the man and the hat. He appeared to be some version of a demon. Maybe a devil? I wouldn't know how to discern what was a devil or demon anyway.

"Become hope. Set them free." I remembered the voices say. *Free from what?* The citizens all seemed like they were living perfect lives, but I wondered if it was all some kind of an illusion.

I was jealous of Copperline children and how they seemed to have everything handed to them whenever they wanted. They had the best schools and books whenever they required them. The city had the greatest and cleanest water. *Why would they need to be set free?*

I was sick of being a spec. I was poked and prodded by syringes sometimes even multiple times a day. I was sick of seeing other innocent specs being tested and beat within an inch of their lives. I hated seeing the seizures and hallucinations of helpless children.

I knew the government was using a new vaccine to try to take people's emotions away. I remember Mark calling it the 'Memory Lane Serum.' They would test it on the specs to perfect the formula. I wasn't sure how many, but Mark told me a number of specs had died from irresponsible over-dosing. Mark believed the mayor had plans to eventually bring the serum to other cities throughout the country and begin a process of expanding Copperline, or at least Copperline's pattern of leadership.

Therefore, I despised the mayor. He was the one causing all this and must've tied himself to the man in the vision I had. I wondered, was Copperline actually a good place, or are the people just as trapped as I am with the rest of the specs? Could they be holding people here as hostages? Maybe the illusion of safety is what kept people here. Or perhaps, it was fear that captivated the people's minds.

I couldn't be the only one wondering what was beyond those walls? For me, I wondered if the hell I was living on this side of the wall, would be any different from the other side of the wall.

Was it the law which gave the illusion of order? Wasn't the law made for the lawless? Of course, the law was for the unjust? Was the law a schoolmaster for murderers to be brought to justice? However, the chief lawless people that I perceived were the ones making the laws.

I didn't know where these thoughts and revelations were coming from. It was almost as if after the thing touched my arm in the cave under the tree, did something to me. *But for what? Why is this happening? Was that the change that Jacobs was talking about?*

I knew it was only days before they got the formula right. All for the mayor's benefit and everyone else's debt.

I laid there in the silence as I wondered what the answers were. If what I read in the old stories about Elohim were real, why would the Maker allow me to go through this? *Why would He cause people to suffer so much? I need answers!*

"You have the answers within your heart." I was suddenly startled by the break in the silence. The voices came from nowhere but were all around me. "I've placed within the power to heal."

"What am I supposed to do?" I asked.

"Become hope. Set them free." The voices seemed to be mocking me.

"You've said that, and I don't know how to do that! Right now, I'm a motionless body on a hospital bed in containment. I'm not worth it! I'm only a spec. Send someone else!" I screamed and wanted to cry, but I didn't have the natural abilities to create tears at the moment.

"Follow your heart, and don't be tempted by those lies." The voice said.

"Why can't you just do this on your own? If you're such a powerful and majestic being, why can't you just make everything right again? Are you actually powerless too?" I asked.

"My power works through those who choose my ways. My power is divine, and it is found in the willing. Don't be fooled by earthly wisdom or power which is finite and broken." The voice spoke with such a thunderous and majestic tone. It demanded respect, yet sounded humble and kind.

"Why does it seem like the good are always overpowered by evil?" I felt that I would confound the great voice in the atmosphere. If I was forced to grow up enduring all that I had, then how could there be more power in the good? It was apparent to me throughout my history, there was greater power in the evil things around me. "Are you good?"

The voice thundered and vibrated through the space as it laughed. It seemed like thousands of other voices started laughing along with it.

"For what is good and what is bad? They're merely your perception of reality. You have endured all of this, and it is making you into a new person. You are Daniel. You have been named after the one whom I called and commissioned to Babylon in the ancient days. He remained steadfast and true." The voice spoke without hesitation. It was like a whirlwind, but also like a whisper. It cracked like lightening hitting the earth, but also how I imagined a father talking to a son. It was the type of voice where if I had breath in my lungs, each chamber would be void of air."People chose to give power to the fleshly things in their lives. For some, it's easier to walk in darkness than to walk in the light of the truth. You give power to whatever force in your life that you feed. Which force will you feed, Daniel?"

I waited to respond. I still didn't know what to say. I wanted to be angry and curse at the great entity, but something else within prevented me from doing so.

"You don't have to speak, Daniel. I will lead you. Pride must be shattered. Love must flow out of you and into the people. Just as the sun is not selective of where it shines, your love should not be selective and judge. Light must extinguish even the darkest caverns of every soul." Every time the voice spoke, a sphere of light grew at a distance, and was moving closer to me. It radiated bright white and yellow light.

Plasma? Fire?

"Look within yourself, Daniel and pull the power from your spirit, like pulling light from the darkness."

"Were those people in the cave also called?" I needed to know why I saw those people tied up by the roots of the trees. I wondered if I should've allowed myself to have been sucked into the earth, instead of going up against this vast evilness.

"They made a choice to be overcome by the enemy. They decided to not use their given abilities for a greater purpose. You made a choice to surrender and escape the enemy now twice, but be prepared, he will come for you again. You must make the choice to remain steadfast and true. Become hope. Set them free." The voice hammered into my ears as the sphere was practically consuming me now.

I was being overtaken by the light. It was both good and frightening. I started to see colors and shapes that have never existed before. They appeared in front of me like I could touch them, but every time I tried, they moved and changed into a different form and pattern. The thousands of voices in the distanced echoed with laughter again. "He can see us," the said as they laughed.

"Why a spec? Why would you use a spec?" I yelled.

"Because of your innocence. I will give you strength when you're weak. I'll give you wisdom when you need it most. I'll give you light in the darkness." I could now feel the vibration every time the voice spoke, but not in my body. I could feel the great entity speak in my spirit.

"How can it be that easy?" I screamed out.

"It will *never* be easy making the right decisions, but it will be worth it, Daniel." I still resisted the light and I suddenly began to feel coldness surrounding me. I felt pain from my head to my feet.

I could feel my body coming back out of comatose. I could feel again my stammering and shaking body slamming against the mattress underneath me. I could feel my arms and my legs straining against nylon straps again. I could feel my torso and chest burning. My head was pounding as if I had just awakened from another testing session with the doctors. I slowly and hesitantly opened eyes, but I was immediately stricken by the bright fluorescent light fixture in the ceiling. They burned within my head, so I clenched them tightly.

Still shaking, my ears became alive to the sound of my own screaming. My mouth was filled with an overwhelming taste of my own blood. My jaw had felt like someone had kicked me.

— C —

Martin watched the body of the spec come back to consciousness. He stood without even the slightest movement, hovering over the shaking body and looking at it in disgust.

"What a shame. It bit its tongue." He shook his head in disapproval.

"Mayor, remember. It had the strength to break one of those straps before." A nervous David watched as Martin leaned in closer to the subject.

Martin turned to look at David through the cracked glass. "You fear like a little child, David. It's not very becoming of you." Martin brought his gaze back to the body. "Besides, we are not here to pick a fight, but only to talk."

Martin slowly straightened his back again and crossed his arms as he waited for the body to stop shaking. He was curious of its eyes. Its eyelids were stammering, but whenever they were open they showed a brilliant shade of bluish green.

Lifting his gaze to another bed in the room, he looked at the lifeless body of Mrs. Roy who passed about an hour ago. He admired for a moment, the fist-sized gash that left the woman's jaw hanging loose. He remembered riding behind a siren-less medical cart that carried the lifeless body.

He could've said that he saw Mrs. Roy wandering in the park and she began to go into shock, but that certainly wouldn't explain the broken jaw and the fractured ribs.

Hardly matters now, she lives alone and people are expecting her to pass soon. I've got other issues to deal with right now.

The spec's shaking and stammering was diminishing. He listened to a few screams that annoyed him, but he looked past it since he needed to have a rather practical conversation with the subject.

"By the way, Doctor, your serum looks as if it's starting to work exceptionally well." He looked at David again who was watching a computer monitor displaying the spec's vitals. "The two medics today never questioned my behavior or poor Mrs. Roy's unfortunate passing. I'm glad now that you and Tom decided to go ahead with the trials this morning."

David kept his face on the monitor and said, "Thank you, Sir."

"You keep up this, Jacobs, and I'll let you call me Martin again." He grinned as David avoided lifting his head.

Martin watched as the shaking body came to a sudden rest. He watched the eyes and mouth open. Its head moved around violently as it tried to actively identify its surroundings. The spec made eye contact with Martin and noticed the lifeless body of Mrs. Roy in a similar hospital bed.

“Its eyes, Jacobs. What color were they before it ran?” Martin said as he looked at the spec.

David pulled a chart from beside the computer monitor. “Brown, sir. Like all the other specs. We don’t know why they changed.”

“Welcome back.” Martin could tell that the spec was in a great deal of pain. *This is going to be easy,* he thought to himself.

— C —

When my body came to a rest, and I finally stopped shaking, I saw the mayor standing over me. His dark gray blazer was exactly as I had seen in many pictures of him.

“Welcome back.” He looked at me with no expression.

I didn’t say anything. I couldn’t manage to get my voice to do anything. I felt the bed move into an upright position. I could see Dr. Jacobs from the other side of the glass watching a monitor.

The mayor held a glass to my mouth. “Have some water. Let’s talk.”

In no way was I about to drink anything that man would gave so I turned my head and starting moving my jaw and tilting my head back and forth.

“Fine, have it your way, Spec.” He threw the drinking glass across the room as it shattered against a wall. I listened to the sound of tiny fragments hitting the floor.

I looked again to see what Dr. Jacob’s reaction would be, but he stood in the same position. However, I noticed another silhouette of what looked like a man behind the doctor.

“Daniel.” I managed to spit out. I coughed up a little blood on my hospital gown.

“I’m sorry?” Martin leaded in toward me.

“My name is Daniel.” I avoided eye contact with him. “Not spec.”

"You have not been issued a name. You are the property of Copperline. A specimen used for testing. And a lousy specimen at that. Your only job was testing, and you failed miserably." His voice was completely opposite of Elohim's. It was obnoxious and making my head pound more with every word he said.

He started pacing and walking around the room, talking to me as if he was talking to himself. "I guess that renders you fairly useless. We could just let you roam around the outside of the walls to see how you make out. Or we could just kill you. We could turn you into a criminal who tried to jump the walls, and you fall to your death. That could potentially be a useful news broadcast for us to use as propaganda. No! I don't like it, because they'll think there are more criminals in the city. So, pretty much useless."

He started laughing as he looked at me sitting there helpless. "But despite how useless you are to us here at Copperline, I want to make a deal with you." He cracked his knuckles and started walking toward the other body. "I want to set you free, Spec. Isn't that what you want? Freedom?"

I sat there and listened. I was mostly too exhausted to talk or react. I stayed motionless.

"I know that within you is this desire for freedom. You want to live and act like a man. You would love nothing more than to put on a suit every day and feel respected. To feel like you're accomplishing something. I know, because I feel that every day of my life." He spoke to me as he looked at the other body.

I remained silent, still feeling my heart rate come back down.

"I can give that to you. I can grant you what you need." He looked back over to me. "I can give you a social security number, an identity. I know you want respect and affirmation, to feel like a man. There is nothing like a woman to make you feel like a man and I can give you countless women. I could give you the money to do whatever you want. Spec, I could give you power."

"At what cost?" I asked. *Was this the test that Elohim was asking about?*

"No cost to you. All the cost is on me. You, spec should look at it this way, I'm investing in your future. I see great potential in you." He started to walk over to my bed again.

Why is he changing his tone? He just called me useless a moment ago.

"Daniel, you say?" His back was toward me. "I like that. I could use an associate with a spine, Daniel. Dr. Jacobs who is cowering behind the glass has suddenly lost his." He started laughing.

"Why haven't you just killed me?" I asked as I watched him slowly turn toward me.

He looked at me right in the eyes. "Is that what you think I do? I just kill people when I don't get my way?" He laughed again, v and dramatically, his voice changed. "What did he say to you down there?" He paused and didn't move a muscle.

"Down where? The tree, or the visions?" I asked. It felt as if he could actually read my mind.

"Visions?" He leaned in. I could smell his obnoxious cologne. "Did he mention me? Did he offer you the same thing?"

I wondered now if he had been referring to the man in the hat or Elohim. *I have to bluff.* "Maybe he offered me something else. Why should I tell you?"

This angered him. I could see his jaw muscles as he started to grind his teeth. "But did *he* mention me?" A dense silence came between us.

Suddenly, I felt tiny electrical pulses beginning to increase in the air. *What is happening?* I saw his eyes widen and go completely black.

"I need you..." He inhaled deep and I knew he was getting ready to scream. "To tell me!" His voice was piercing as he shouted right into my face.

I said nothing as a jolt of electricity pushed my body against the mattress.

"Did he say anything?" When he shouted, the foundation of the containment room shook. The lights flickered and dust fell from the ceiling.

I set there still. Mostly not knowing what I should say, but then I remembered that Elohim said he would transfer strength and wisdom to me. I looked at the straps that were holding me in the bed. I broke them before, but I also remember the pain associated with it.

The mayor stepped back and grabbed something from a table to my right. It looked like a heavy duty nylon strap. I'd seen those on pallets when the transport trucks brought in supplies from outside of Copperline. Thick, yellow straps with large metal hooks on one end of the strap and a large metal ratchet already fed through the clasp and ready for use.

"Spec, I hear you're well-read. You may have been reading books that were smuggled in by our medic friend who passed yesterday." He came toward me and dropped the strap and ratchet down on my gut.

I said nothing. I only grimaced at the heavy ratchet hitting my stomach.

"See, I'm missing a book. One that you may have already finished, but it has been misplaced and I *need* that book." His voice went from a normal tone to the ear piercing yell again. "Where's the book, Spec? I need to know!"

Again, the room shook and the light dimmed, but I said nothing. I watched the mayor become insane. His emotions went up and down as fast as a seesaw.

He collected himself and paused. He straightened his tie and fixed his jacket. "Tell me spec. Do you know what *poena cullei* refers to?"

I couldn't remember reading anything that contained those words.

He smiled. "See, in 100 BC, if one was found guilty of murdering their own father, which *you will* be tried and found guilty."

"Father?" I stammered.

He tilted his head, almost in delight, as if he was enjoying this. "Oh yes. Did I forget to mention?" He looked at the glass and turned back. "Mark Waters was your donor. You, Spec, were the twin of their eldest son." He started laughing. "They didn't even know you existed. That's how good I am. What an ironic twist. Your escape attempt caused his death."

My eyes started watering, and rage was building inside of me. This whole time, my father had been right there. That would explain why I had always felt such a connection with him. I wondered if had known.

"Anyway." The mayor started wheeling the other body over. "In the days of old, they would've sewn you into a sack with snakes, a dog, and a rooster. You can use your imagination as to what happened. I have none of those, but I do have this fresh corpse that I acquired earlier. I am going to strap you to poor, old Mrs. Roy and let her decaying dead body eat yours away."

I started whispering, "Elohim."

He leaned in and looked at me with disapproval. "I'm sorry, not even God Himself will pull you out of this. You have a decision to make, Spec. Follow me and join *us* by taking an oath, or rot with this disgusting carcass." He bowed his head and held his hands in a praying motion. "May the prince of darkness have mercy on her soul."

"I'll never join you. I will destroy this hellish city! Copperline will burn!" I screamed at him with everything I had. When I did, I noticed the ground shaking and the lights bursting above us. Sparks began falling all around me, almost as if they were falling in slow motion. A burning smell filled my nostrils. I noticed a cloud of smoke or a fog-like substance begin rolling through the air. I felt all the tiny hairs on my arm and neck stand straight up. I clenched my jaw tight and breathed through my nostrils.

He looked back at me dazed and confused. Thousands of hot pieces of glass from the fluorescent light were falling everywhere. More sparks flew out of a nearby outlet. The two men from behind the glass quickly hit an alarm. One of them ran to the glass where the intercom was.

"Martin, get out of there!" The other man said loudly. "His pH levels are rising!"

I sat there with my eyes fixed on Martin. The only light in the room was from the glow of the control room on the other side of the glass. A single security light flickered on behind me, but quickly burst when I pictured myself destroying it in my mind.

The Mayor scowled at me. I could smell something difference from him. The terrible smell of cologne was gone, he now emitted the smell of fear.

"I'm not finished with you." He snarled at me under his breath. "If you think you can come into my hospital and disrupt me, you're mistaken! You're terribly wrong!" Then more quietly, almost under his breath, I heard him curse and say, "this is *not* over."

Martin stood up straight and walked over to the body on the other bed. He grabbed the end of the bed and threw it into the glass. The lifeless body went through the air like it was a rag doll.

I was disgusted, not only by his lack of character, but his disrespect for what once was a living being. I couldn't help the tears that were welling up in my eyes. “I’m sorry! I’m sorry!” I cried out in sympathy. *I should’ve taken his deal,* I thought. *This is all my fault.*

“She’s already dead, Spec! It’s much too late to apologize!” Martin walked toward the door as the men inside opened it quickly for him. “Pathetic!” He yelled as he left the room. I could see him yelling at the two men in the control room, but I couldn’t hear a word that was said.

I looked at the body of the woman on the floor. I pitted her and envied her at the same time. *Why do I have to go through this?*

I have to get out of here. I’ve got to set these people free from this madman and his clowns.

Twelve

Mellissa finished picking up the house. She kept watching the clock in anticipation of the children coming home from school. Her nerves were on edge since meeting X. She knew he must've seen exactly how her husband died, but it angered her that he wouldn't talk about it.

Mark Jr. was now the man of the house, and she just needed him around to make her feel safe. Her husband always had a way of making her feal safe and secure, but now the task would be up to her son.

She kept driving herself crazy with all the thoughts running wildly through her head. She could swear she kept smelling the mayor's ridiculous cologne, but she didn't know why all of a sudden. She despised that man's scent. *It's almost like he was here. Come on, Mellissa, get out of your own head!*

She made several trips to the basement to finish stacking boxes of her husband's remaining things. Boxes that should've gone to the transfer container, but she just couldn't part with them.

She realized the door leading to the bulkhead was propped open slightly. Once again, paranoia crept in. *Did I leave this open?*

She thought. *Am I losing my mind? I really need the children to be home.*

Walking over to the opened door, she shut and locked it. Looking around to inspect the basement again one more time before she went upstairs, she could feel the hairs on her neck stand up. She whispered to herself, “There's nobody here, Mellissa.”

She started thinking about the book again. She was still at a loss as to where it could be, but if the mayor had it, she would certainly never see its contents.

She kept trying to remember what Mark told her about the secrets Martin and his crew were keeping. She wondered again why Mark would choose to stay there if all of those secrets were true.

Mellissa studied pictures from an early photo album of their family together. She found pictures from when she was pregnant with both children. Tears began to fall down her face again. She knew how the recent events were going to change everything. Mark Sr. was gone now, and the other two would be off to college and their careers soon. She wanted so badly to make time go backward just so she could pause it.

Mellissa walked back up the stairs and the subliminal waft of the mayor’s cologne had entered her mind again. She groaned at how much she didn’t want to go to the Hurd Manor for dinner that evening.

She imagined her son walking in wearing his black blazer and blue tie that she watched him put on earlier that morning. Mark Jr. was so handsome. He was so ambitious to get into politics that it scared her. He would use the mayor as an example of how he intended to act. Many of the young men in Copperline High School were driven for success and very polite in manner, but Mark was miles ahead of everyone else. An easy vote for class president. He already attended city forums and had practically memorized Copperline's ordinances and policies.

But Mellissa knew there was just something off about Martin. She certainly didn't hold the same endearment as many of the other citizens did. *There was something a little off about that wife of his too,* she thought.

Mellissa wondered if there was anything real to Sarah. Was she really an outstanding person who gave herself for the welfare of her children, or was Sarah Black just as plastic and superficial as some of the other council wives?

— C —

The time she had finally come for the children to arrive home from school. Jordy entered the house first with the news that she was a potential candidate for a Scholastic Art & Writing Award. Her mother gleamed with pride for her. Considering the recent circumstances, this would be a pleasant distraction for her daughter. Mellissa too, needed a diversion.

Mellissa was always so proud of how strong Jordy was for her young age and often saw her as a public leader, even more than her brother. Jordy wasn't swayed by popular opinion, but instead, she stood up for what she thought was right. Jordy had a great sense of discernment. However, she feared the mayor may attempt to turn her heart toward him, as well.

Mark Jr. finally entered the room and greeted his mother with a kiss on the cheek. "Good afternoon, Mother." He spoke with an enormous smile. "You're looking beautiful, and the house looks great!"

Just like his father, Mark Jr. was a charmer, and Mellissa needed every bit of charm that her son was willing to hand out.

She smiled in return with watery eyes. “Thank you, Mark. That is very kind of you to say.”

“Mother, I want you to know that I will take care of you. We will not have anything to worry about. It’s what Father would have wanted.” Mark stood straight and looked right at Mellissa almost as if he was presenting something to her. “I want to make sure that you never have lack.”

Mellissa smiled even more. “Mark, you’re very sweet. I’m proud of you for stepping up, but your father and I have always been so proud of you both. I’m not lacking anything because I have you, two children.” Though, she was worried. She wanted to retain as much time with them as possible. Without them, she felt there was nothing.

He stood there silent. She could tell that there was more that he wanted to say.

“What is it, Son?” She became curious.

“I love you Mother, and I have wonderful news!” He placed his hands behind his back and stood tall with his chest full of air.

“I love you, Mark. What is your news?” She was wondering why he was announcing his news like this. It made her nervous. Jordy causally came in and talked about her big news by simply slipping her mother a note from the school, but Mark was stopping the presses.

“I was called into the staff and board room today. My teachers and councilors have recommended me for early entry into the Public Policy Training Program! One of the mayor’s associates came in and said how I would be shadowing leaders in the city council as an internship-style program.” He paused, hoping to see his mother’s excitement.

“Why would you do that?”

“Mother?” His face was riddled with confusion.

"I'm sorry Mark." Her heart sunk. She didn't want to hurt him, especially now after just losing his father. "I meant to ask, why would you do that before graduating?"

"The staff said that it was recommended by the city council. They informed me that I could receive my high school credentials early and it'll allow me to start as soon as next Monday!"

He was brimming with excitement and joy, and she was not about to put a damper on that. However, in her heart, she was scared. She wondered if this was somehow a strategic move by the mayor in some kind of chess game.

I want no part in this. He must know something. Why else would this be happening? This is no coincidence. The nervous widow thought to herself.

"Do you feel that it's right in your heart?" She asked him the very statement that he heard from his father ask him on numerous occasions. She also knew, that if he was a man like his father, he would take the night and think about it. She knew that her husband taught both of their children to never make rash decisions.

"I've been planning on this for years, mother. I feel that I'm adequately prepared, and I'm open to the potential this job has to offer." He stepped forward and held his mother's shoulders. "And the best thing. We will never again have to worry about safety or finances."

"I'm not worried about that now, Mark. You protect us, and your father's city pension along with his life insurance will provide more than we need." She said as a slight rebuttal, still trying not to offend her son.

"But this is so much more, mother." He leaned in towards her. "We could move to the townhouse sector. I could give you a kitchen like you and Father always talked about having. Imagine, free health care for life."

She knew that he was starting to feel upset by her response. She pictured him as the little boy he once was, not so long ago. Her heart was broken and touched at the same time. *I just lost your father, I'm not losing my children too.*

He painted a really good picture, but this would certainly hinder her plans to get out of the city. Mark Jr. would never agree to this exodus.

"Mark, I am very excited that I received such exciting news from both of my brilliant children. You both deserve this." She tilted her head as she spoke to him. "The only thing I ask is that you take a night and seriously ask yourself if it feels right in your heart. When do you need to give them an answer."

"It was today, mother. I already did. The mayor needed to know. I told them I accept."

—C—

A large, stainless-steel blade cut gently through the celery on the cutting board. Sarah had been back from the market for some time now. She had started on the dinner preparations in the kitchen while the contractors continued their work on the manor.

She distracted herself with the fantasies of leaving Martin, but she didn't know how she would pull off such a stunt. Getting four children in a cart, while two of them should've been living in a spec dorm, would certainly be an impossible feat.

"Ma'am, we got the windows to open, and have finished turning the old fireplace into a hutch." Henry stood in the doorway of the kitchen. "But for some reason, we can't figure out how to keep those floorboards fastened down. We even put screws in a few ends, but then others popped up. It's almost like your floor is shifting. Maybe the ground is shifting? I'm not too sure. It's an old house and…"

"Thank you, Henry." Sarah stood up straight and put on a polite smile like she knew she was supposed to. The last thing she needed was Henry telling Martin that she was rude. "Strange about the floor."

"Indeed. I really think it needs to be taken up completely and a new one put down, but that would certainly not be done by dinner tonight. I'm assuming that the old boards need to be taken up and replaced with plywood." He started to leave but then turned back. "Also, ma'am?"

Sarah answered, "Yes?"

Henry looked as if he didn't want to say anything. Sarah even thought he was uncomfortable. "My partner got your basement door working, but the smell seems to be coming from your guest down there."

"My guest?" Sarah dropped the knife that she was cutting vegetables with.

"Yes, ma'am. Please, I'm sorry. I don't mean to offend." Henry held up his hand to his chest. "It's just, the smell is…"

"What… guest?" Sarah's eyes were wide and focused upon the carpenter.

"The blind fella." He paused. He looked both confused and worried, she thought. "He was blind, but he certainly knew we were in there. It looked like he was doing some sort of religious meditation because he was lying still in the dirt. We thought he was dead at first, but he…"

Sarah said nothing, but walked to the door and. The subtle creaking sound filled her ears as she slowly opened the door. She stood there silently looking down the dark stairs. She saw the dirt floor of the basement that had been built so long ago.

"Ma'am?" Henry took a step towards Sarah. "Did you not…"

Sarah quickly held up her finger to quiet him.

She studied the roughness of the wooden stairs as she slowly returned her eyes to the bottom of the basement floor. The pungent smell of sulfur increased around her. The light from the kitchen shone around her, slightly illuminating the bottom of the stairs.

Studying the stillness, she felt her heart rate increase in her chest. A slight change in temperature chilled her as she noticed the hair on her arms standing straight up.

Silence. *There can't be anybody down here,* she hoped. *This is just a misunderstanding.* She thought she could hear a slight hissing and crackling noise.

Sarah started her descent to the basement. She felt her body trembling as she loosely grabbed the cold wooden railing. The stair tread creaked as she stepped.

Suddenly, a haunting, dark shadow moved rapidly past the bottom of the stairs. Her eyes widened in horror. An intense shriek unconsciously came from her lips as she stumbled back up the steps and tripped over her own feet. With her arms flailing through the air, she fell backward as her head hit the edge of the countertop on the way down.

A sharp pain from the blunt hit shocked her as the world around her went dim. She could slightly hear Henry beckoning his partner.

-C-

She came to with a large gasp as she felt cold water all over her face. Her eyes opened wide and quickly to see Henry and his laborer standing over her with shocked expressions. "Ma'am, are you ok?" Henry held her shoulders as she tried to regain her composure.

"I'll call the medics." The partner grabbed the phone that was hanging on the wall.

"No!" Sarah blurted as she violently shook her head while holding out her hand. She could still feel her body trembling as she sat there on the floor.

Sarah quickly got to her feet and slammed the basement door shut as she grabbed a chair from the table to wedge under the door knob.

The two men remained quiet as she ran out of the kitchen. She could hear them talk in hushed tones. "I'll call Martin," she heard Henry say.

Sarah ran to the staircase in the foyer. She started envisioning different scenarios where should would leave Copperline.

Could I call the city concierge service and have them bring the car to the manor? No. Martin would be notified of the request. She didn't even really know where the parking garage was located. *Could I try to hide the kids in the back of a cart and drive out of the East Gate? No. Gate security would notify Martin. Could the children and I climb over the wall? No. Martin would get notified of a breach.*

She was stuck.

She was afraid. First of Martin, but now of whoever was living in their basement. And why didn't Martin say anything to her? She didn't even think it was livable down there. She avoided the basement at all costs and only saw Martin go down very little.

She started to feel sick just thinking about all the times she had been there while the two older kids were at school. *How long has he been here?* She started asking herself these questions and causing herself to panic even more.

She felt claustrophobic in the house all of a sudden like the walls were closing in.

She went into Margret's room and waved frantically at her to follow. She couldn't form any words in her whirling state of panic.

"Give me liberty, or give me death." She could hear Bradley in the study reading and readying himself for a school project. She immediately grabbed him by the arm. He looked at her confused.

She took both children and went to a door they had never seen behind. She reached for the key and unlocked the access.

Bradley looked at his sister with a scowl.

"Mother, what is the meaning of this?" Bradley said as he attempted to pull free from his mother's grip. "Why are you acting this way? Where are you taking us?"

Without saying anything, she allowed the kids to enter first and she made sure the contractors weren't watching. She tried to control her breathing as she was on the verge of hyperventilation. Sarah watched both of her children walk in front of her, make their way up the narrow and dimly-lit staircase.

Bradley looked back her as if he was very bothered by her actions. "Did Father approve of this? Why have I never been here before, Mother? Mother?"

Margret looked back at her mother concerned. She reached out to hold Sarah's hand. "Mommy?"

"You can't talk like that, *Margret*." Bradley snapped at his sister. "You wait until Father hears of this."

Sarah put her finger to her lips and stared at Bradley. He stood against another door in the narrow staircase.

"There's something you both should know." Her heart was pounding. She pushed the same key into an old lock, but she noticed the door was already slightly ajar. She held on to the door and turned to the children.

Bradley looked at her, still upset that he was taken in such haste. "What *is it,* mother?"

Sarah pushed the door open and watched Bradley burst into the attic. "Wait, Bradley, there's…"

"What, mother? What do you want us to see? There's nothing here."

Thirteen

I laid there strapped to the bed. It felt like it had been a great deal of time since Martin left the containment lab. He spoke with the other two men behind the glass before I noticed him exit. The two other men stayed for a maybe two or three minutes before they exited.

There I was, stuck in silence. Just the corpse and I. For what good company is a corpse? Not great company at all, but still slightly preferable than the mayor.

Mind you that when bodies are without life, they begin to emit a terrible odor. I didn't know how, but I could imagine this unfortunate woman being in the wrong place at the wrong time. *Rest in peace, ma'am,* I said to myself. She was free from this madness.

I had to break out of this prison. I know that I'd attempted so many times, but I'd failed each time. There was something different. I felt some sort of strength that wasn't there before.

I wasn't sure what to make of the foreign idea of strength. I've read articles of women lifting cars off their trapped children. I've read stories of war heroes that exhibited superhuman abilities all due to some kind of scientific anomaly. Was that it? An anomaly?

I wanted to think that it was some sort of superhero ability. However, I hadn't been bitten by a radioactive spider. I hadn't consumed some green ooze that turned me into a mutant. I'm just a lowly spec who was apparently separated from my twin sibling at birth.

A spec. I cursed. That whole idea made my skin crawl. My dorm had 9 other specs just like me. They were all somebody's son. Some were younger, some older. And in the girls' dorm, those were all daughters. We were the lost children. We didn't know where we belonged in the world, outside of the spec dorms. *Will we ever meet our parents?*

A mother. The thought felt great, but it seemed like this unrealistic dream. I had been alive for 17-25 years based on my growth patterns, and I'd lived every single one of those years with the given knowledge that I had no parents. *Was Mark really my father?*

I wondered all the time if I'd ever get to meet my mother. I wanted to believe that there was at least a shadow of possibility. *There has to be a possibility,* I felt my stomach tighten as I thought that with deep emotion. The idea of meeting her inspired me to move. It energized me to get out of this jail cell.

I remember the doctor saying my pH levels were increased when I exhibited great strength. I remember Elohim told me that He would give me strength. Was that part of it? Was this scientific anomaly or divine strength?

Either way, I had to try.

I tightened my arms against the nylon straps. I could feel my muscles starting to flex. I slowly started trying to pull my arms up and rip the straps.

Nothing.

Come on, Daniel.

I tried again, but this time applying more physical strength. *Nothing.* The nylon straps were not budging.

I rested for amount and searched deep within myself. I closed my eyes and inhaled deeply through my nose and held my breath for as long as I could before I exhaled.

I've got to give myself a reason to break these straps. Daniel, Imagine yourself free. I've got to envision myself breaking them. I've got to remember how evil the mayor is and how he needs to be dethroned. Become hope. Set them free.

I tried again. I closed my eyes and inhaled deep and held my breath.

I exhaled.

I repeated a long and deep inhale.

Hold.

Exhale.

I repeated this until I felt like I was going to pass out.

Then with every bit of muscle and might that I had, I tried to lift my arms out. My teeth were grinding as I grimaced. My voice started to growl.

"Elohim!" I groaned. And then decide to give it one last push. "Give, me, strength!"

I felt like my eyes were going to bulge out of my head, so I closed them tightly. I started coughing. I felt like I was going to be sick. I started to listen to the sound of tearing straps as they began ripping from my arms and legs. My head was throbbing with pain. I heard a voice screaming, but I quickly realized it was my own. I felt my arms and legs break free. I had been separated from the bonds which held me down.

I felt a euphoric sense of relief wash over me as I allowed my body to rest against the mattress.

What next?

I sat up in the bed and looked around. I looked through the broken glass to see if I could see anybody. *No movement.*

I slid my legs off the side of the bed and slowly stood to my feet. My legs were a bit cramped from the muscle strain as well as the stasis I had been in. I pulled the heart monitors and other wires off of my upper body. I pulled the IV out of my hand. It started to bleed, so I grabbed some gauze from a table next to me and wrapped up my wound tightly.

I hobbled over to the door.

I had watched a few people enter and exit through the door at the time I had been there. I didn't know what to expect on the other side of the wall, but I couldn't let that sway me from my exodus.

I tried to punch in a few numbers on the lock panel of the door. Nothing. A single warning came on the screen that denied my access.

I inhaled deep and long.

I imagined what freedom meant to me.

As I exhaled, I pushed hard against the door. The panel malfunctioned when the door slid open just enough to allow me to pass through. I ran to the other end of the control room.

Next objective. Find clothes.

I couldn't just run out of the room with a hospital gown on. I needed cover. I needed to somehow get to the medic's locker room. There must be clothing in there. I wondered if I could disguise myself as a medic or a guard. I was much too skinny to be a guard, but I thought I could've passed for a young medic. They only had standard issue black cargo pants with white polos. *I really could use a hat too.*

I tried to remember what Mark used to wear. *Did I look like him?*

I connected with Mark so well, that when X had killed him that day, I felt like a part of me was stolen. He was my friend and we had so much in common. We wrote often. He had me put most of the letters in the books he lent me so we both wouldn't get caught. Our shared connection would certainly make sense if he was my father.

I made my way to a door. It wasn't a sliding door like on the other end of the room, but it had a lever like it was a simple closet door.

I turned the lever handle slowly and quietly. There was no light on the other side of the door. I pushed it slowly and carefully, until the door was open. It was a dark closet with medical supplies.

I turned on the light and saw that it was more than just a closet. It was a room that was lined with microscopes along the table tops. *It must be a lab,* I thought. Large white filing cabinets were side by side along the wall. There were four large steel cages that had thick metal bars. The door of each cage was unlocked, but one of the enclosures looked like it had been damaged by whatever was locked in it.

Whatever was kept in there had to have been incredibly strong to bend those bars. I brushed my hand over some kind of bite or tear marks in the metal. I wanted to look more into it, but I had to find clothing.

I noticed a door in the back corner of the lab. *Another door. Closet?*

I rushed over to find it slightly ajar. I pulled it open slowly. I found a complete supply of clothing! Medic uniforms, lab coats, nurses' scrubs, and even a few utility hats with the Copperline city logo on the front. *Perfect.*

I quickly grabbed a medic uniform and a utility hat and changed. I had no idea when the other men would return, so I needed to get out of there fast.

Making my way back into the control room, I approached a glass sliding door next to the containment lab that I was being kept in. I tried to open the door manually, but an error message appeared to my left on a digital access panel.

I pounded the access panel in frustration and a light slowly faded up inside the room. As the area became illuminated, I saw several bodies lying in hospital beds all connected to monitors. Then I recognized them when I saw the man with bandages wrapped around his hands. These were the nurses and medical workers in the containment room when I shocked them all somehow. This lab was almost identical to the one I was being kept in.

They all appeared to be unconscious.

I looked to my left to see another door with a lever. I turned it slowly and began to open it just enough to see light coming from the other side. I couldn't hear anybody. I had to make a move into here. I assumed light meant sun. Sun meant outside. Outside meant freedom.

I was shooting from the hip and hanging on hope. I had no knowledge of this floor. I had no real knowledge of anywhere except for my dorm. My only idea was to follow exit signs and try not to be noticed.

I slipped out of the room and into the brightly lit hallway. I also had a sudden dark realization that I would be on camera. The city had cameras everywhere and that thought haunted me. I knew that I had to quickly find a crowd. Mark told me that the cameras were so small, someone wouldn't even expect there to be a camera watching you, but there most likely was. He also said the only place in the city that had minimal cameras was the East End, because of the rushed development.

I need to find a crowd. Where? How?

I suddenly had a thought come over me. *I need to create panic.* I needed to get people moving toward the exits. Once there's panic, I could jump in the crowd and go unnoticed right out the exit.

Look for the opportunity within chaos.

I crept slowly down the hallway. If anybody was watching on video, I was toast. I needed to think fast. *How do I create panic?*

I didn't see anybody until I walked further down the hallway that fed into a lobby. I saw a few people waiting and talking to each other. Others had their faces in a book.

How do I do this? I turned back toward the control room to see if I could acquire something to use when I saw out of the corner of my eye, Dr. Jacobs approaching the door.

I didn't have much time. I looked around. Something bright caught my eye. *Fire alarm. Perfect.*

I pulled the alarm.

There it was. The sound of my freedom sounded like a terrible, high pitched siren. Strobes started flashing everywhere. The calm and pre-recorded PSA layered over the siren started repeating, "Please remain calm, and find the nearest exit. Please remain calm, and find the nearest exit. Guards will be able to assist you if needed."

I grinned as I watched people widen their eyes with surprise. They jumped up from their seats and sprang to their feet. They immediately started running toward a hallway that had a bright red exit sign just beneath the ceiling. I found my way out of here.

I followed a large crowd of people who were running towards the elevators. Only a few elected to wait for the elevators while the rest sprang quickly into the stairwell and started to descend.

A guard jumped out of nowhere. I cursed. *Did he see me?* "Everybody, please calm down! The elevators are disabled durning a fire emergency."

I joined the stair crowd. *I don't think he saw me,* I said to myself.

Nobody here recognized me. Just another face in the crowd. A face who wouldn't even know how to recognize himself.

It was almost comical to see these people acting like this. Grown men were plowing over women and children. Where was the honor in that? Where was the chivalry? A few men in the crowd spoke up and told them to remain calm, but no such result was attained. I had never experienced anything quite like this. I had no idea what to expect, but I got a kick out of it, nonetheless.

I listened to the sound of hysteria. The people shouting at each other, the sounds of people's shoes descending the stairs, and the slight echo of the guards trying to get everybody to remain calm. *Remain calm,* I laughed as I said that in my head.

Finally, we all descended to a ground level where there was suddenly a view of green grass and a stone walkway through a glass door.

People began bursting through the door. Still the sounds of the siren and the flashing light of the strobes were adding to the chaos.

I was just about to the door when I happened to look behind me. With all the commotion, I completely forgot that Jacobs was about to walk into the containment lab when I pulled the alarm. He was about ten or twelve people behind me.

Did he notice me? It doesn't matter, I thought. I was younger. I was lighter. I didn't think I'd have a problem out-running the old man, but I'd still prefer to go unrecognized.

A mass of people in front of me started filtering out through the door. Pushing over one another, they squeezed through the door. Some children were crying, which I felt guilty about.

As soon as I got outside, I looked around and realized that I had no idea where I was going. If I started to run, would I draw too much attention to myself? I needed to find a tree line or an alley next to a row of buildings to escape down into.

People were everywhere outside. A few just started to leave, but most everyone was still standing looking at the building. I slipped out from the door and found a large group of people to get into.

I listened to the murmurs of people asking each other where the fire could be located. Others were worried about loved ones still inside the building.

I watched Jacobs exit the building as well. He immediately looked back and up at the building. I ducked down behind a taller man in front of me, but I kept me eyes glued to him as he pulled something from his lab coat. It appeared to be two vials. He held each up to the sun and then turned his head in my direction.

Did he see me? Does he know? I had to make a move.

Jacobs turned and placed the objects back in his pocket. He then walked slowly and casually around the corner of the building, out of sight.

If he knew I was there, why didn't he chase after me? *He must not have seen me,* that's the only reasonable explanation I could think of.

I had nothing around me that looked familiar. I looked to my left as I walked away briskly. I saw a small tree line that led to a row of townhouses. That was my best bet. That was my only bet. I snuck out of the crowded area with very few people watching me, but most of them turned their attention to the oncoming firetrucks.

Turning my brisk walk into a jog, I headed toward the trees. I looked behind me to see the gap I created between myself and the building. I needed to find a place to hide, quickly. Mark mentioned that he lived in the newly expanded sector. I remembered him saying the streets were actually paved with black tar in that area instead of the decorated stone in the city square. I knew I had to look for the black tar roads.

I often wondered why he told me so much about the location and description of his home, but I then wondered if he was actually preparing me. I also wondered why a man like Mark would stay in Copperline when he knew about the corruption in the city.

Was this all part of some divine purpose? I shook my head as I ran. *No, it couldn't be like that. This is all just a mistake. I'm just a mistake. No, I'm not a mistake!* I stopped running for a moment and put my head in my hands. I was so confused. I was lost. I was becoming a crazy person.

I need to find my mother, I thought. *Will she believe me? Elohim, give me wisdom.*

— C —

Dr. David Jacobs made his way back to the containment rooms after stopping at the lab to pick up a new serum that the alchemists had been working to perfect. A new formula, referred to as Memory Lane. David thought of its potential as he walked. It was designed to be a drug powerful enough to wipe existing memories and to clear a slate for a new cognizance to be programed into the patient.

David knew that if the spec wouldn't talk willingly, it needed to be drugged. He also knew that it would expect David to enter the containment room with a loaded syringe, so he decided to send the serum into the ventilation system of the Containment Room. They had created this option for vaccinating multiple patients during the measles outbreak. *A contained airborne vaccine.* He grinned at the hopes of restoring the trust between him and Martin.

The Doctor was almost back to the lab when he noticed a man in a medic uniform in the hallway. He didn't want to be seen by anyone knowing what he had to protect in his pocket.

He started to open the door to lab when strobes and sires began to alarm. He cursed. He turned and exited the lab. A number of panicked people started running through the hallway next to him. One of the vials fell out of his coat pocket and on to the floor when a man was shoved into him from the panic. "No!" The clinking sound of glass hitting the floor was more nerving than the alarms to David. "Please, watch out!" He reached for the vial as someone kicked it as they ran in front of him.

The Doctor watched as the vial bounce hard against the wall and floor. Ducking and weaving in between people who were running to the exit, David pushed people as they ran past him. "Stop!"

He bent and picked up the vial and started jogging with the rest of the crowd. He got to the bottom of the stairs and exited through the same glass door that everyone else was exiting through. David looked up at the building in confusion as he took a couple steps onto the lawn.

He took the vials out of his pocket and held them up to the sunlight. "Should be fine."

He looked over at the crowds of people and wondered if anybody would notice if he went around the corner of the hospital to sneak his way back inside to check on the spec. He quickly ran next to the brick facade of the building as he came to a corridor access that was left ajar. Looking around and not seeing anybody paying attention to him, he darted back into the building.

The Doctor briskly walked down an empty corridor that led to the same stairs he just descended. A few people were still exiting the hospital, but he tuned all that out as his concern was getting back to the containment room.

He approached the lab entrance and walked inside. He immediately noticed the light to the other containment room was on. *Strange,* he thought. *Maybe the fire alarm set off the motion detection?*

Then he saw the door in the first containment room slightly opened with the screen flashing 'ERROR' in bright red lettering. His heart sank.

Fear turned his mind to mush. He couldn't think. His head spun in too many different directions. He knew this would be the last straw.

He quickly ran to the door and looked through the glass. An empty bed with broken straps. He cursed. "Martin is going to kill me."

Fourteen

Martin stood over three bodies all sleeping soundly in a hospital room. One adult male, and two children. He watched as the IV dripped into a tube which would fill their veins full of Pentobarbital. They would remain like this for as long as he needed.

The Mayor convinced himself that he needed to do this. *Sarah needs to be remember just how much control I have,* Martin thought.

The doctor came into the room. “All set, Mr. Mayor?”

Martin stood massaging his chin with his hand. “Yes.” He paused and directed his gaze toward the doctor. “It’s a shame that they all have the same blood disorder.”

“Very much a shame, sir.” The doctor smiled as he spoke. “Just let me know how long I should keep them like this.” The doctor said as he held a clipboard under his arm.

“And remember. Sarah is never to be allowed in this room.” Martin said returning his gaze to the bodies. “I will see to it that she never learns about this hospital room," he mumbled under his breath.

The doctor reached out his right hand and touched Martin's shoulder. "What room, Sir?"

Martin looked and smiled as the doctor nodded and left the room. He walked over to the body of the adult male and touched the sheet over the foot of the patient. "It's good to see you, Father."

Martin felt no remorse. He felt no pain. He was angry. He resented his father for not allowing him to be more involved with the public policy when he was younger. While his father said he wanted to protect the young child from the corruption.

It was Martin's idea to create the serum that caused blood disorder. He needed to get his father out of his way so that he could march down to the Citadel and take his rightful place as Mayor of Copperline. He quickly became the corrupt person that his father feared.

He started to walk out the door when he heard the alarm and saw the strobes in the hallway. He rushed out to see chaos. Nurses were rushing to get patients into their rooms. Most were keeping a composure, but some became panicked and started to cry. Patients began to look around in confusion and fear as they started to question what would happen to them.

"What is that?" One patient said as they tried to make their way up from a wheelchair.

Martin walked over to the man. "Sir, it's Mayor Black. I'm sure this is just a drill of some sort." He helped the man back into his chair and walked briskly over to a computer at the front desk.

He logged into his surveillance application remotely and started searching hallways and lobbies. No smoke or fire, only people panicking everywhere.

"This is going to be a mess to clean up," he sighed to a female nurse next to him.

The nurse touched his arm. “What should I do, Martin?”

“Just have everyone try to remain calm. I can’t see anything here that looks like an immediate threat. It’s got to be an error of some sort.” Martin kept searching camera feeds all throughout the hospital. However, there was only one feed he cared to see at the moment.

He felt anger instantly flare up in him as if his skin had caught fire. Something in him knew this alarm had to be related to the spec. It irritated him that people were panicking. It especially irritated him that the nurse was still standing there with her hand on his arm.

“Now, Veda.” He snapped at the nurse who had been watching over his shoulder.

As the nurse left and started directing people back into their rooms, he brought up a couple camera feeds that were labeled authorized access only. He entered his code and it brought up a poor quality image of Dr. Jacobs looking on in disbelief at the empty containment cell.

“That’s why.” Martin shut the application off and stood up. “Nurse! Nurse, Veda!”

The nurse turned and looked at him. “Yes?”

He started shaking his head. “Have these people pull it together. It’s nothing more than an accident I can confirm there is no fire. It looks as though a fire alarm was inadvertently set off.” He lifted his head to yell to the rest of the people that were surrounding him. “There is no fire!”

“Okay Martin,” Veda said as Martin made his way to a security control panel.

Martin pulled the security panel up and entered his pin code to silence the alarm. He also wanted to see which alarm was triggered. Not to his surprise, it was the alarm next to the containment lab door.

He found an empty closet and slammed the door shut. Martin pulled out his mobile device and dialed David.

"This is… Jacobs." He heard David's shaky voice answer.

"Tell me exactly what you know." Martin wanted David to sense the anger in his voice.

"I just returned from the alchemists' lab with the new serum when I heard the alarm sound." The phone started to break up a bit as David spoke. "Someone hit me as they ran through the hallway. The impact knocked it from my hands to the floor. It… It got away from me. I got it back in my, but I had to exit with the others. I… I couldn't have made it back through the crowd anyway. When I got outside, I inspected the vials. I made it back in as soon as I could, but the spec…"

The line was silent. Martin wanted David to feel the weight of his animosity. "How long were you gone before the alarm was activated?" Martin asked.

"Look, Martin. Tom and I were doing what *you* asked." Martin knew that David was grasping for things to say. He stuttered as he spoke to his mayor. "It… It couldn't have been more than 20 minutes. We all agreed for us to do this. I heard the alarm as I made it back to the lab."

"I don't need you to remind me of what *we* agreed to do. Don't try to push the blame, fool." Martin wanted his voice to pound into the phone like a hammer against the doctor's ear.

"The medic!" David said.

"The medic?"

"I think I remember seeing a man that resembled Mark Waters, and I…"

Martin couldn't contain himself anymore. His laughing interrupted the Doctor. "You thought you saw a man who looked like Mark Waters, and you did nothing?" He cursed into the phone.

"They all…" He sighed. "They all look the same." David stammered out.

"Pathetic!" Martin screamed into the phone. The lights in the closet dimmed as he yelled. Static came over the phone. Martin had finally lost his patience for this man's incompetence.

"I'm so-" David tried to say before his neck involuntarily snapped back and this body grew limp and hit the hard pavement floor of the containment lab. Martin could picture it in his mind. A sudden release came over him as he heard the sound of David's neck break and his dead body hit the floor hard.

Martin lifted his head to the ceiling and sighed with his eyes rolled back. He ended the call and exited the closet.

As he entered the hospital hallway again, he casually adjusted his jacket.

The Mayor stood up straight with a polite smile on his face. "I'm terribly sorry, everyone! This is really embarrassing. Someone had triggered an alarm, and we have dealt with it accordingly." His face smiled as to put everyone who saw him at ease. "There is no need to panic. I assure you that everything is under control."

People nodded in relief. Some even started to clap. Martin radioed the Hospital guards and cleared the building for reentry.

Veda watched as he took control of the situation. Martin met her eyes and titled his head toward the back of the room. She walked over to him. "Well, that was interesting," she whispered.

"That's not the least of it. Can you get this place back in order? The spec…"

She smiled as she looked into his eyes. "Sure thing, Martin. We've got this. You have plenty to take care of. We can talk later."

Martin smiled at her as he touched her chin and turned to walk away. He could sense her heart beating rapidly.

Martin walked into a nearby service corridor where he could get out of sight. He pulled his mobile device from his pocket. He noticed a shadow approaching him. Veda quickly followed him into the vacant space. Before he could say anything, she kissed his lips.

"Veda," he said as he pulled back. "Not here…"

"Shh," she brought her finger to her lips and smiled as she quickly left the area.

Martin lifted his head to see a security camera panned away. He sighed and shook his head as he dialed Tom.

"Black," Tom answered.

"Meet me in the lab."

— C —

Sarah sat there in the attic while her two children watched her cry. The children were trying to console her. Margret asked her what was wrong, but Sarah simply and pathetically didn't know how to respond. With one last exhausted sob, she realized her need to stop her evil husband. She didn't know what to make of whatever it was that she saw in the basement. Her heart was filled with fear and regret.

"He did this." She cried out to the children, but she knew they wouldn't understand. Sarah grabbed hold of the two of them and held her children.

She wondered if the contractors would've left the house by now. The last thing Sarah thought she heard was that Henry was going to call Martin.

Martin. She hated him so much. He would be home soon and the dinner was not even near ready. She had only a few short hours before she would be hosting another family from the city, and she would have to put on another facade.

She couldn't take it anymore. She wondered if Mellissa was like the other pretentious citizens in the city. She desperately needed someone to talk to, but feared she was alone.

Her breathing was labored and her chest felt as if someone had stabbed her. All this fear and stress would eventually kill her if Martin didn't first. She hadn't had the benefit of breathing easily for years. She was constantly afraid of saying or doing the wrong thing.

"Mother, stop this behavior, at once!" Bradley pulled away from her embrace. "Shouldn't we be going downstairs so you and Margret can prepare for the meal?"

Her heart broke. Martin had him trained already. Sarah had even seen signs of Bradley becoming more violent in the past year or so.

Margret started to whine, "Mommy, I…" The little girl was interrupted when Bradley slapped her face.

"You address her as, Mother. That is proper! Has Father taught you nothing?" He stood over her like Martin had done with Sarah so many times before.

Sarah scowled at her son with outrage. "Now, that's quite enough out of you!" She grabbed her son's arm.

He pulled it away immediately and scowled back at Sarah. "You just wait until Father gets home."

She sighed and thought to herself, *I have to get my children out of here. I have to get Bradley out of this environment where he can learn how to be a true gentleman and not another one of his father's puppets.*

Sarah shuddered at the thought of going downstairs. What was that, living in her basement? She didn't want to be in the house anymore. She looked around the attic again, as if it would bring back her children that he must've taken somewhere. *Where did you take them?* She wondered what he did to them, and hoped they were safe. Chills ran down her spine. She knew exactly why he took them. Leverage.

"Let's go downstairs." She hated saying those words. In her mind, her subconscious was fighting against her instinct. "We have lots to do tonight before your father gets home."

She would manage for tonight, but she needed to begin finding her way out. *I'm done with this hell hole!* She screamed inside her head. She wondered more about Mellissa. Perhaps a door can be opened there. She would've preferred leaving on her husband on her own, but if there are allies amongst her, she should find out. She wondered if there was a place she could run to. *There has to be a place within the city that Martin doesn't know about,* she thought.

As for the other children, she didn't know what to do. Martin has tunnels all over this city, all protected by his codes. She wouldn't even know where to look. She barely knew how to get to the East and West gates. Not to mention his marionettes he had all over the city, were painfully faithful to him. She didn't actually know who she could trust.

Sarah and the children started to make their way to the attic door. She turned the knob and allowed the children to exit first. Suddenly a rush of cold air ran up through the stairway and into the attic. It wasn't like a rush of cold air from the freezer being left open, this was something that ran through her and chilled even her soul.

"Mother?" Margret also felt the rush move through her. She looked at her mother with a frightened look on her face. However, Bradley kept his face forward.

"Please keep going, *Margret*," Bradley said in a stern voice. "You and Mother have to prepare for our guests."

"Bradley, did you not feel that?" Sarah had asked her son, startled that he didn't react in any way.

"That's just Asmodeus. He does that every now and then." Bradley said with no emotion at all in his voice. "He's been growing. That's why the floor is popping up."

"Bradley. What are you talking about" Sarah was alarmed. What had her son been doing?

"Before Father boarded up the fireplace in the dining quarters, he and I would talk." He paused. "But we wouldn't talk using our mouths, we would talk using our minds."

Sarah didn't know what to say or do. She didn't even know what to think. "He's growing?"

Bradley tilted his head. "Yes. I think it's mostly because he's eating. He said something like he feeds on bad words that grownups say."

"Do you still talk to him?" Sarah had to ask.

"He's asking *me* why you are asking all these questions." Bradley turned and frowned at his mother and pushed his way around Margret.

Margret looked at Sarah with tears in her eyes. Her skin became void of any color. The both of them were in disbelief at what they were hearing from Bradley.

Bradley reached the bottom step and turned. "Mother, we shan't be tardy. Father will become angry."

Sarah stood for a second contemplating her options, but she quickly realized she had none. She motioned to Margret to follow Bradley.

"But Mother?" Margret whined.

"It's okay, honey. We'll figure this all out." She bent down on the step so she could whisper to Margret. "Look at me. Mommy will figure this out. Everything will be ok. *We* need to stick together. Please, promise me that you'll stick with me."

Margret looked in her mother's eyes. Sarah held out her pinky which was trembling. Margret curled her pinky finger around her mother's.

"Now let's go make dinner for your father and our guests." She smiled at Margret.

Margret wouldn't budge. Sarah picked her up and carried her down the rest of the stairs. Sarah could hear her muffled sniffling and crying as they walked through the door and onto the 3rd floor. She felt warmth again. A tiny bit of relief gave her enough courage to keep moving forward.

They descended to the second floor when Margret ran off to her bedroom and shut the door. Sarah didn't blame her one bit. She wanted in the worst way to join her daughter and hide out there.

Bradley informed his mother that he would continue his research for his school project in the living room.

Trembling, she made her way to the basement door in the kitchen. She studied the door knob as a shiver went down her spine. She looked away and saw that Henry left a note on the counter.

> *Mrs. Black, I finished up what I could for today. I went to check on you after you got back on your feet, but I wasn't sure where you went. I left a message to let the Mayor know to check on you when he returns home.*

She put the note back on the counter and saw the knife and the vegetables right where she left them. She reached across the counter and started to rinse them off again. She needed to keep her mind off her son's odd and troubling news.

She wondered if he had been possessed by whatever this thing was. She was never religious at all, but she remembered her husband and her brother-in-law talking about an oath. Sarah remained quiet on the phone line while listening in to the brothers' conversation.

*I better check on him again, s*he thought. She walked into the Great Room to find Bradly quietly reading in a history book. Without making a sound, she looked at him just as he snapped his head up at her. "He wants to let you know that he always watches you. He really likes it when you sing."

Sarah gasped and quickly ran back into the kitchen. Sick to her stomach and suddenly without air, she fell to her knees. Dizziness overwhelmed her as she held her face in her hands and started to sob. Sarah was terrified at whatever this thing was. *How could it watch me? I only sing when I'm in the bath.*

An overwhelming need to vomit possessed the frightened woman. Rushing into the bathroom and kneeling at the toilet, Sarah started dry heaving.

She set back on the floor of the powder room trying to catch her breath. Martin would be walking through the door at any moment now.

Get up, Sarah. Get up and pull yourself together. You're a mess. Pulling herself up and standing face to face with the mirror to reveal that her face was without color at all. Eyes, red and swollen from all the crying would not be preferable to Martin.

Sarah began to apply the make-up with trembling hands. Her whole body was shaking. "Come on. Pull it together," the housewife said fighting back tears.

Finishing her make-up and returning to the kitchen, she resumed cutting the vegetables. People began gathering at the end of the driveway. She studied the crowd through the kitchen window and wished there was some way that Martin wouldn't come home today. *That's ridiculous. He'll be here soon.*

Sarah carried the duck from the refrigerator to the counter and pulled the cutting board out from under the island. She could see the great room from this angle. *Where was Bradley?* She asked herself.

Entering the great room cautiously, the timid housewife became white with fear again and rushed up the stairs to Margret's room to check on the little girl.

Margret was there on her bed in a pile of blankets. The tiny girl had created a fort-like pile that barricaded her from everything going wrong in the house. For many reasons, Sarah envied her little daughter and wished she could join her in there.

"Margret, honey." She took another step inside the room.

She listened and finally could hear a faint, "yes mother."

"Is Bradley in here too?"

"No," the tiny voice was a huge relief.

Where's Bradley? Sarah left the bedroom and slowly ascended the stars to the third floor. Her right hand trembled as it slid on the wooden railing. Without going all the way up the stairs, she witnessed Bradley gathering more books to help him memorize facts for his project.

Bradley, sensing his mother looking at him, sighed. "Don't worry Mother, He's not talking to me right now."

Standing silently and looking hard to see if there was anything strange about the boy, the hesitant housewife was quivering. He still looked like the precious little boy that used to bring home flowers from the garden in the park. "Is that so, honey?"

"It is. He left. He also wants me to stop telling you when we talk, so I have to honor his word." He looked at his mother and shrugged slightly.

"But you shouldn't talk to strangers, honey." Sarah didn't know what to say, but out of instinct that was the only thing that came to mind.

Bradley looked at her and looked confused. "There are no strangers in Copperline, but only neighbors."

Martin has got to him.

The sound of people clapping faintly became like an alarm sounding though the thin stained glass on the driveway side of the study. She made her way over to the window to see the crowd welcoming Martin.

Sarah closed her eyes and sighed. *Here we go.*

Fifteen

Mellissa was disappointed to hear her son's news of the early entry into the program, but he had his mind made up. She was most disappointed at the fact that he didn't talk to her about it first. There was no searching his heart for the answer, which was something that his father always tried to teach him before making any major decisions.

His focus was set and it terrified her what he was about to embark upon. If her husband knew secrets and was sworn to secrecy, how much more would a member of the council come to know? She knew that there was no way her son would be as open to her about the things her husband was.

She had finished getting ready before the children. Jordy didn't take a shower, but only freshened up. Mark had just gotten into the shower after completing his early achievement and release forms from the high school. Mellissa knew that she had to sign them as well, and there was no convincing him otherwise. He had worked hard for this, and in a way she was so proud of her son.

She entered his room and smiled as one of the first things on his desk was a picture of the four of them from one of their Sunday moments together. Mellissa's heart was full of love at that moment. She was going to miss everything about Mark Sr. Mostly his ability to always bring the family together.

She was scared that by losing her husband, the ability to keep the children's interest in her would start to dwindle. They were so intelligent and ambitious, and ready to take the world.

On his desk, was also the paperwork from the school. It stated that he cleared an open interview with a Thomas Black. *The mayor's brother,* she said to herself. She did not trust that family one bit.

As she stepped around to the side of the desk, her foot hit her son's book bag. She didn't think anything of it and continued reading the papers that she would need to sign. She picked up a pen and sighed deeply as the pen hovered over the paper.

Mellissa looked down to see the backpack that she hit with her foot. Noticing a few things had fallen out and also creating an effort to stall with the signature, she picked up the items that spilled out of his bag. Casually placing the things back in Mark Jr.'s bag, Mellissa noticed the title of the book *The Art of War.* Her heart jumped. Anxious and excited, her eyes widened at the sight of what she was holding.

Mark entered the room with a towel and noticed that his mother was in there. "Mother?" He looked surprised to see her in there. "I would've brought the papers down later."

"How did you get this book?"

"Why does everybody want that book?" He looked at her confused. "Doctor Black was asking if I knew anything about it as well. I know it's on the unapproved list, but I couldn't let him know that Father gave it to me."

Mellissa untied the leather strap that was holding it together and pulled a bunch of papers from the back of the book. She flipped through the pages. She pointed at notes that her husband left in the margins. "This is why."

Mark Jr. stood silently with a puzzled look on his face.

"Mother," Mark whispered. "What would happen if people knew we were in possession of this?"

It was almost as if Mellissa couldn't hear him. She had been hoping this would be in their possession before the mayor. She was suddenly joyful and hopeful for the first time since Mark Sr. died.

"Mother?" He reached down and looked at the folded pieces of paper that his mother placed on the desk. Some were layouts of the spec dorm. One of the papers had counts of children who were donated by unknowing parents, both male and female. Another small piece of paper contained a brief description of what a testing specimen was. One list contained donors' names. Mark's eyes became wide as he focused on one piece of paper specifically that had fallen to the desk. "Mother."

Mellissa was searching every page trying to taking it all in. The notes in the margins were heavy with information concerning something her husband referred to as 'The Others.'

"Oh, Mark." She whispered to herself.

"Mother, you need to see this." Mark handed her the paper with names of people who had unknowingly donated one of their twins for spec use.

Mellissa grabbed the paper while still searching the book. She slowly lifted her eyes to the paper in her hand. She looked at Mark who was pointing at the paper. She directed her eyes to the paper again to see her name on the paper.

"Mother, that's my birthday." Mark's voice was shaky. "What does that mean?"

Mellissa put a hand over her mouth. It all was starting to make sense. She felt that she was pregnant with twins, but the hospital was very clear that it was only one child. She suddenly felt that she understood why her husband kept them there all this time when she wanted to run.

She started to shake her head as tears filled her eyes. "Mark." She couldn't make any words. Her breath was labored and her heart was stinging with pain.

"Mark," she felt like she was going to be sick. "Did you tell anyone that you had this book?"

"No! I told them that I'd never heard of it." Mark spoke softly. "I can't believe I lied to them, but I wasn't even going to tell you. I…"

"Ok, thank you, honey. We need to hide *this* information," she pointed to the loose papers she found in the back of the book. "But the Mayor wants this book."

She held up her hand and looked at her watch. The dinner was less than an hour away. She stood up and directed Mark to the bathroom. "I don't know if we're being watched or listened to." She ran the hot water of the shower and the sink to steam up the air and create noise in case they were being listened to.

Mark with a curious look questioned his mother's actions. "Mother, what are you-"

She held up one finger interrupting him. She leaned in toward Mark Jr. and whispered. "We need to give the Mayor the book tonight at dinner, but I need to keep the papers that I found. The mayor can't know about the papers. Can you keep this a secret?"

Mark looked at his mother. "I would do anything for you, Mother, but there's something you should know."

She looked at him nervously.

"Tomorrow for my second psych evaluation, they will be giving me truth serum while connected to a polygraph monitor." Mark's words sent cold shivers down her spine.

What do we do? She sighed. *Okay, don't panic. Stay calm.*

"We'll talk about this more tonight after the dinner with the Mayor and his family." She paused for a moment. "But for dinner, we need to attempt to regain any trust we may have lost since the mayor found some of your Father's journals. If we turn the book into him, but we keep the papers, it may appease him. He doesn't need to know about the papers that your Father left for us."

"He told you specifically that he was looking for this book?" He brought his hand to his forehead.

"No, but I know that he tore out that page in your Father's journal." She was trying to remember all of the details of the meeting last night. "On the page, it must've mentioned this book. We don't need this, we only need the loose papers. I'm assuming that he only knows about the book because he senses a threat. This will buy some time."

He looked at her again still with a sense of bewilderment. She could tell that he was still trying to process all of this in real time.

"Look, Son. We'll turn it in with the other books. I'm sure we won't be in trouble since your Father was the one with the books. We can play dumb." She looked into his shifting eyes. She could see his nervousness. "In fact, this will make us outstanding citizens. I'm going to hold on to the papers, but turning in the books is what's right. Can you do this for me, Mark?"

Mark hesitated as if he was trying to formulate something to say. "But mother." His eyes searched hers. "I also will make an oath to serve and protect our citizens and this is unacceptable behavior for me. It was unacceptable of Father to behave like this. We should tell Mayor Black everything. Won't he understand?"

She started to shake his head. “No, Mark. I’m sure that he would *not* grant us grace if he knew that we had this.” She held up that pile of papers. Her eyes begged Mark. “We are doing the city a great service by turning in the books.”

He nodded slowly and bit his lip. His eyes were still wide and full of fear. “I just hope I can-“

“You can, Son. I know you can keep this a secret at least for tonight during the dinner. I’ll present him the books, and we will play it off as a nice evening with the first family. I’ll explain how I found these controversial publications while going through more of your father’s possessions.” She spoke with more confidence than she felt.

He nodded again. “Ok. You’re right, but I’ll need to know what to do about tomorrow.”

She kissed her son on the cheek and left the bathroom.

— C —

I was lost. I was running through unfamiliar territory. The sun was going down and whenever I saw lights from carts, or people out for a jog, I would find a place to hide.

The houses were labeled with people’s last names on a plaque on the sidewalk in front of each house, but I couldn’t find one that said ‘Waters.’

The street lamps started to turn on slowly. I was sure that cameras were all over this city, and by now, news about my disappearance would certainly be known to the proper people. These cameras would find me in due time if I didn’t formulate a plan. I needed to find my family and develop a strategy for defeating the enemy. A strategy to take down the most powerful man in the city.

I thought about my family and wondered if they knew anything about me. I wondered if I looked like my twin brother or sister. I wondered what I looked like in general. I had only seen faint window reflections all my life. Dark hair, I know that much. I haven't shaved in two days, so probably a little scruffy. At least, I felt scruffy. Beards were only allowed to be grown in the winter months. I didn't know what month this was, but by the way the sun was setting, I didn't think it was winter. I had to shave every day regardless of the date. Specs don't have the same allowances as citizens.

I saw a treeline ahead, so I darted towards it. I figured it would be harder to make out a person in the trees. It would be dark soon and since I was sans flashlight, I needed a place to rest for the night.

Plus, a treeline was indicative of the wall. I need to get over or through that wall eventually.

I kept thinking of that quote from the *Art of War* that I borrowed from Mark. There was one quote that was burned into my memory banks for eternity.

"The supreme art of war is to subdue the enemy without fighting." The sentence rattled through my brain. I felt like I wanted to fight the mayor. I wanted to defeat him with my own two hands. I also wondered if the true art of victory wasn't in violence, but in a greater peaceful solution that allowed the truth to reign.

I was still trying to wrap my mind around everything. Was I ready to expose the city's government?

An approaching light forced me to jump into the trees. As I hid there, I couldn't help but wonder if each person I saw outside of the hospital were family members. At least I knew my father, and I got along with him and we enjoyed each other's limited company. I'm very thankful for the time I spent with Mark.

The cart passed on down the road, but I decided that I should walk through the woods from then on. I kept an eye on each light post. I realized that the tinted bubbles under each light-pole were most likely the video cameras. Avoiding those would be in my best interest.

I needed to somehow figure out where I was and where I was going. The only thing I knew was that I needed to look for the tar streets. I remember he mentioned smaller housing too.

I came upon a path in the woods. It looked as if the people started to make a road, but never completed it. Or, perhaps it was a road that was going to be used for future expansion. Either way, I didn't see any light poles with cameras. *It may have to be good enough for tonight,* I thought.

I made a plan to walk for a little bit longer, but I was losing energy from all the adrenaline rushes and emotional rollercoasters of the day. I was hungry. I couldn't remember that last time I ate.

Not that the specs got to eat regularly anyway, but something was better than nothing. Some days we would go without anything more than just a single portion of protein, and a tangy glass of warm water. Sometimes I wondered if they served specs the runoff water from the other residence. I was wondering if that's why they referred to it as 'gray' water. It didn't look too gray, but if I had to associate a taste with gray, it would've been that nasty water.

I wish Mark lent me something that would've helped me more outside of the spec dorm. Living outdoors was not something within my knowledge base. However, it came with an extreme amount of magic and wonder. The smell of fresh air was almost euphoric. Walking with the sound of dirt underneath my shoes was such a great sound. I loved how the long blades of grass felt on my fingers. Once the sun went down behind me, it changed how things looked in the sky. Perhaps, it was only the way I saw perceived in the absence of light, but the change was excellent. I started to witness stars appearing in the sky for the first time in my life. I was overjoyed.

I continued walking until I came to an opening where the tree line ended. It looked like an old part of the city that they left abandoned. The buildings were behind me and a field that was maybe twice the size of the cafeteria in the dorms appeared in front of me. Other than waist-high grass that had been kissed by the sun, the field was barren. The rising moonlight was illuminating the desolate area around me.

The scent of the ground around me was intoxicating. I stopped walking for a moment and stood in the quietness. I closed my eyes and stretched out my arms.

Is this what freedom feels like? I inhaled deeply. I felt safe there.

Beyond the field, I could see the wall. The trees in this part of Copperline weren't very tall. I rested silently against the trunk of a tree, watching stars become more visible in the stratosphere. *It's brilliantly beautiful,* I thought to myself as I watched the sky become like a backlit canopy with tiny holes punched in it. I couldn't help but smile at the beauty of the night sky. I felt myself drifting to sleep, but this time without the aid of the drugs they would give to me. This was the sleep that I welcomed.

— C —

The Waters approached the gate of the Hurd Manor. Mellissa's stomach was in knots. Mark Jr. was silent all the way over. Jordy sat in the back seat of the cart while her brother drove his family. It was an awkward silence and a strange emotion between the mother and son. Jordy was picking up on the peculiar tension.

Mark stopped the cart and hit the intercom button at the front of the gate.

Right away, Mayor Black responded. "Mrs. Waters and family! Please come on in!"

Mark cleared his throat and replied to the Mayor. "Thank you, sir."

The gate of Hurd manor started to open slowly. Mark sighed and looked at his mother. She returned the look with a simple smile.

Jordy tilted her head in the back seat and winced. "Why are you two so weird tonight?"

"Language." Mark muttered as he looked at his sister in the rearview.

"What?" Jordy sputtered. "Is weird a bad word now?"

"Please don't talk to Mother like that."

"Like what, Mark? I'm only asking a question. It's obvious that something is wrong." Jordy spoke as she watched her mother just sat in her seat remaining composed. This made the girl nervous.

"You don't think we're making a terrible mistake do you, Mother?" Mark Jr. payed no attention to his sister's remark. He started to accelerate the cart.

Mellissa touched his shoulder. "Let's go have dinner with the Mayor, Son."

Jordy set forward in the back. "Mother? Mark, can you please tell me what's going on?"

Mellissa only looked back and smiled at Jordy. She held in her hand three books that she hoped would appease the Mayor. She wanted to ward off any future interrogations.

The family stopped at the florist prior to their arrival at the Hurd Manor. Mellissa made a bouquet of Orange Gerberas. With flowers in one hand and three books in the other, she stepped out of the cart once her son brought it to a stop.

Jordy was amazed at how beautiful her mother was. She wore a blue skirt with a pearl white blouse that was astounding. She was always amazed at how her mother could gracefully wear any outfit she wore. The girl wanted to be more like her mother in that way.

The three of them made their way up the beautifully constructed steps that looked exquisite with the yard lights illuminating every row of granite. Even the grass that edged the stone was the perfect length and the perfect shade of green. Each row of flowers were almost more beautiful than the previous. The Manor displayed many different species of flowers that set the yard apart from any other property in Copperline.

Mark was the first to the door. “Should we knock?”

“Unless you can open the door with the force, Jedi.” Jordy snickered.

Mark Jr. knocked on the door.

Jordy stood there, disappointed of her brother’s lack of response. “That’s all you got?”

Mellissa looked at Jordy and nudged her with her knee. “Shhh.”

The large wooden door opened. Mrs. Black greeted them. “Good evening, Waters family.”

Mellissa didn’t like how plastic and rehearsed she always seemed. Nothing about it was normal. Was her life really that perfect? She wondered what would happen if she slapped her in the face for no reason whatsoever. Of course, she would never, but she wondered things like that.

“Hello, Mrs. Black. Thank you for having us tonight.” Mark’s voice was soft but very pleasant as he walked into the house. “The Hurd Manor is absolutely beautiful. We are blessed to be seeing it with our own eyes tonight.”

Jordy silently walked in. Her father always taught her, if you don’t have anything pleasant to say, don’t say it at all. She cared more about retaining information that would be useful later, than having to apologize because she hurt somebody’s feelings.

— C —

Mellissa smiled and handed the flowers to Sarah. "Thank you, ma'am. As Mark said, your house is absolutely astonishing."

"Thank you, Mellissa." Sarah received the flowers, but also leaned into Mellissa. "I'm looking forward to getting to talk to you," she whispered.

Mellissa looked at Sarah and nodded. This confused her and threw her off guard. *Was this a sign of humanity? Was she real after all?* "I would like that."

"Well, I can see that everyone is getting acquainted," Martin said from the other room. He entered the foyer as he looked at Sarah.

Sarah smiled at Martin and walked into the kitchen.

"Mayor Black, it is an honor to be in your home." Mark offered his hand. Enamored by the mayor, it was as if he couldn't contain himself. "I accepted the early entry for the PST program today!"

Martin shook his hand. "That's great news, Mark. We've seen much potential in you, and I'm hoping we can talk more tonight."

Mark's eyes were wide with excitement allowing his mother to see that little boy in him all over again. "That would be incredible, Sir. I want to learn everything that I can from you."

Martin looked at Jordy and offered his hand for her to shake. She politely shook his hand. "Good evening, young Jordan Waters who I hear just got news today of a potential award. It' because students like you, Jordy who continue to light up our program at Copperline High."

Jordy politely smiled. "Thank you, Mayor Black."

Martin moved to Mellissa. "Ma'am, thank you again for accepting our invitation. We are looking forward to getting to know your family."

Mellissa shook his hand. "Thank you for your kindness and your hospitality this evening. We are also looking forward to the dinner. This house is-"

"A headache and work in progress." Martin interrupted. "We had a contractor in today, but we still have miles to go. We apologize for the floor which is finally falling apart after *sixty-eight* years. And our propane line smells from time to time, so again we apologize."

"No need, sir. It's astonishing." Mellissa encouraged herself. She thought she was doing great at laying it on thick tonight. She watched as Mark and Jordy went into the other room.

Mellissa leaned in and lowered her voice. "Maylor Black, after you left the other night, I found these books in my husband's collection. I wanted to do the right thing, and make sure they ended up in the right hands." The widow watched as the mayor's eyes instantly became wide as he saw the publication, *The Art of War.*

"Why, yes… Yes, ma'am. Thank you so much for bringing this to me. I really do appreciate this."

"Of course." She smiled. "And I really appreciate you and your team working with Mark Jr. in the program." She forced herself not to choke on those words.

"We are *really* looking forward to working with him. He really does show quite a bit of potential at such a young age." They both began walking into the dining room. "Both of your children do. I know you must be proud."

"We are." She caught herself, and she instantly felt sick again. "I'm sorry, I meant I am." She composed herself quickly. "Speaking of children, where are yours tonight?"

"They are… tied up tonight. We wish they could've been here, but they are away."

Sarah was listening and watching out of the corner of her eye from the other room. She kept wanting to get Mellissa aside and actually talk to her. She needed someone desperately, but she was worried about the items she just gave her husband. She couldn't quite make out what they were, but seeing his reaction was cause for concern.

What was that? She wondered as she took the duck out of the oven. All she could do was think and worry about were her children. Two of them were tied up in the attic, and two of which she had no idea where Martin was keeping them. She was forcing herself not to shake, but she was panicked inside.

She was indignant at her husband and how he could keep such a posture and appearance despite everything he puts her through.

Martin entered the kitchen. "How's dinner coming, Sweetheart?" He said intentionally in a loud and boisterous manner, making sure his guests could hear him. The mayor placed the books down on the counter and grabbed three wine glasses and two drinking glasses from the cupboard.

Sarah looked at the top book cover out of the corner of her eye. "Just about ready, Dear." Her voice wasn't quite as loud, but she made sure to remain pleasant. "What are those, Martin?" Sarah pointed to the pile of old books.

Martin walked to the refrigerator but waited to respond until he was next to his wife. He lowered his voice. "Maybe she is more on our side than we thought. She found banned books that her husband owned and wanted us to have them so we could destroy them. I find that kind of integrity, refreshing." He looked at his wife with a disgusting look.

Sarah had learned to ignore most of his snide remarks and looks, mostly because if she did even head fake in the direction of addressing it, he would lose it.

She was forcing herself to be the Sarah that everybody knew and most envied. Chipper and prompt. “Finishing touches, Dear. Would you like spicy, or tangy sauce for your side?”

— C —

Martin found his wife’s attitude quite pleasant, which was a nice surprise based on her disobedient behavior when he arrived home after the office. Sarah had become quite mouthy when she refused to be along with him so he decided to punish his wife by keeping the children bound in the attic with a dosage of sleeping medication.

But this was like the Sarah of old. This reminded him of when they first met, and she thought he was the greatest thing to ever happen to her. Sarah had always acted like all the other women in town around Martin, but she was the one that caught his eye at the time.

Martin was also very delighted with how Mellissa was treating him. Perhaps he really was wrong about her. She handed him the books with such politeness. He wondered if she had looked at any of it. *Why would she have gone through with the dinner if she had?*

Then he paused. *Unless, of course, she has read it and got what she needs?* He picked up the book and quickly thumbed through the pages. It looked like Mark had underlined and circled parts of it. Some heinous comments about poor leadership frustrated him, but he wasn’t too worried about those.

“Maybe I’m overthinking this, but he did mention The Others.” he mumbled to himself. “But why would she so willingly hand this over to me, unless she truly *did* trust me?”

“What was that, Martin?” Sarah held up the side sauces.

"Nothing. I'll take spicy." Martin said, distracted by his thoughts.

— C —

Spicy, was exactly what she was hoping for. She made the sweet sauce for everyone else. Whatever this book was, it was distracting him, and he would never even notice the amount of sleeping aid she mixed into the sauce.

Her conscience wouldn't allow her to do anything harmful to him, but she wanted a chance to spend the night in the attic with the children. Martin had been so unpredictable lately, that she didn't want to be around him.

Sarah put the sauces with each specific plate. Keeping the spicy sauce for Martin in a white bowl, while the other sauces in the brushed nickel bowls. She noticed how Martin was still distracted by this thoughts. She could tell that he was stumped. Martin wouldn't be baffled though. As smart as that man was, he would not be mislead. He would always get to the bottom of the matter somehow.

— C —

Mellissa stood in the dining area while her children were in the next room marveling at the lovely house. She was enthralled by the workmanship of the hutch in the dining room. Such a lovely and intricate design. It looked modern, but also matched the character of the house.

Mellissa often remembered the work her father, a carpenter did when she lived in Massachusetts. She remembered many happy times watching her father work diligently in his shop. Earl Becker, her father would work from home during the nights creating intricate designs for stair rails, hutches, and wardrobes. She would quietly watch him work to create something beautiful from the most formless pieces of oak, maple, or cedar.

She loved the smell of cedar. The hutch reminded her of something her father made, and it instantly filled her with nostalgia. Mark and Earl got along so well and that not only led her to think about her father, but also about her husband.

Martin entered with three wine glasses and two drinking glasses on a lovely brushed nickel platter. He placed it carefully on the table as he noticed Mellissa studying the hutch. "It was newly installed today."

"It's magnificent." She was still studying and appreciating the craftsmanship. "My father was a carpenter before he retired. He also used to make furniture like this. I really love the attention to detail here."

Martin walked over to where she was standing and also began to study it. "I can give you the name of our contractor. He does all the work on our home. He's the best and the only man I trust to do amazing work, and complete his work in a timely manner."

She smiled as he walked out of the room and returned to the kitchen. She tried not to breath through her nose around him. There was something about his cologne that was completely offensive to her. She remembered it from somewhere, but couldn't put a finger on it.

Mark Jr. saw his mother studying the hutch in the dining room and joined her as Martin returned to the kitchen. "It reminds me of your grandfather's work." She smiled at Mark Jr.

Mark instantly started whispering. "Do you think we did the right thing bringing those here?"

Mellissa held her finger up to her lips as she looked softly at her son. She winked at him.

The widow had spent the short time had at her house, not only reading some of the random notes that her husband put, but she also added a few random notes. Some jottings were completely random that had nothing to do with the book, or Copperline for that matter. Her plan was to try to throw off Martin to the point where he would begin to think that Mark was not a threat at all.

She also began to think of a few benefits of having Mark Jr. in that program. Maybe there was a silver lining there. She wondered if her husband was able to have a little role in the government and maintain his integrity and character, then so could her son. She only wanted him to avoid making any oaths that were done in private.

She knew she would be playing a dangerous game here, but one of the greatest truths in that book reminded her to "appear weak when you are strong, and strong when you are weak." She whispered the sentence into her son's ear.

She would be ready for whatever came her way.

Martin and Sarah stood in the doorway to the dining room. "Dinner is ready!"

Sixteen

I sat there falling in and out of sleep, somewhere along the tree line of Copperline. I was a little surprised that I didn't hear guard dogs, or people searching for me. I knew that there had to be people watching the cameras looking for me, but even though it's a gated community, I was told it's still one of the largest cities in America. There's quite a bit of land to cover.

I tried to take in consideration how I found myself going through a rabbit hole like Alice in Wonderland. I shivered, not because of the cool air, but because of the oddness of the situation that plagued my memory. I was partially delighted at my momentary freedom, while I was also conflicted.

Maybe I should've taken the Mayor's offer. I should've taken the money and the power. I've never known what money can do for me and a large part of me wanted to experience the life that the Mayor offered me. Would that have been so bad? "Set them free," I remembered Elohim instructing me. *But was that really Elohim? Is any of this actually real? Why am I questioning Elohim?*

However, an even bigger interest of mine, was finding my mother. I wanted to see what she looked like, and maybe what she sounded like when she talked. I wondered what her name was.

I began to feel overwhelmed. Being hungry, tired, and scared were just a few of the right ingredients for a breakdown. I slumped further down at the base of the tree where I was sitting. I curled up into a crouched position and held my head against my knees and I started to cry.

I didn't know what I was doing, and I willingly admitted that then. Despite how much I wanted to know my family, I imagined climbing the wall and running away from the city completely. However, I had no knowledge as to what was beyond that wall. For all I knew, it was just a continuation of what was in front of me.

I started to pound the ground and grumble in irritation. Questioning myself wasn't helping anything, and I realized I needed to stop, but I remained frustrated. Having a fit and boxing the ground was only making my hand raw.

Out of sheer exhaustion, I finally started to doze off. I could feel my eyelids getting heavy. I could feel my breathing changing, and I welcomed the overwhelming feeling of falling asleep. I knew if I didn't fall asleep, I would work myself into a panic attack. Perhaps after rest, I could continue on in my journey. I resolved that I would attack one thing at a time.

I fell asleep as I leaned back against the tree facing the field.

I immediately started to see visions of Bodie again, but this time it was like I was only watching, and not actually there.

I was watching four people who were knelt down before the man with the hat. However, the man looked different than he did when I saw him in the previous dream. He looked almost as if he were a black cloud-like figure. He still kept the shape of a man, but there was something extremely not life-like about him.

The four people who were knelt before him were unrecognizable. I couldn't see their faces, but they were muttering something. It was something in another language that I couldn't make out.

I tried to pay closer attention to see what they were doing. Three of the men started to stand while one held his posture. I wondered who they were. It appeared as if they were taking an oath. The man would say something, then the three men would repeat it.

"Now rise, my children." The man with the hat touched them each on the shoulder as they began to rise. One of them stepped forward and said something to the cloud-like figure that I couldn't understand. The man with the hat laughed and breathed upon the subject. I looked again to see that it was the Martin.

With a stream of black vapor being injected into the mayor, he also screamed as the man breathed into him.

I looked at all the men. The one in the middle also looked like the mayor, and the other man was Dr. Jacobs. The mayor and the man who looked like him were standing straight, while Dr. Jacobs' head was hanging.

Suddenly I saw the man in the hat finish breathing into the mayor. He looked over at the Doctor and pushed him over. "Such a shame, Martin. He could've been valuable to us."

Martin? Us? I continued watching and wondered who the fourth man was, still kneeling. The man with the hat walked over to the kneeler and started to examine him.

I looked closely, and the fourth man was trembling violently. I couldn't tell if he was crying or if he was seizing. The man spoke to him. "And you... You, my child, will be next. I will breathe fire into your soul and you will wreak havoc over them that try to come against us."

Then the devilish man walked over to the man standing next to Martin. “Did you, Thomas, destroy the Tree of Life?”

“I did, Master.” Thomas looked straight forward as if he was being called upon by his drill sergeant.

“Silence!” With a vulgar and rancid smell, the man opened his mouth wide when he yelled. He screamed with a volume that shook the ground. “You did not destroy the tree! You merely brought it down. I found the spec in there!”

Martin stepped forward again. “I’m taking care of it, Master. His brother will also lead us to him eventually.” Martin pointed at the quivering body still kneeling with its face to the ground.

Brother? Could this be my twin brother? Has he turned himself into this dark monster? Has he taken the bait?

The man began to laugh with an unfathomable sound. A sound so evil that it shook my core as I continued to observe this seance.

“And what about his mother and sister?” The man looked at Martin and waited for him to respond. “What will he do about them?”

Martin responded, “He and my son will work together to destroy all those that come against you, my Great Lord.”

As Martin spoke, the man arched his head back and threw his arms wide. Fire rose from behind him and the black smoke-like figure turned to fire.

Tree roots all around them were turning into snakes that started biting at each other. The branches began to burn the leaves that were hanging off of them. The sound of drums began to fill the air around me. The sky turned a dark red, almost as if the sky was smoldering.

The two men still standing bent on one knee as the man with the hat breathed on them again. This time with fire. It was always Martin that received a double portion. Dr. Jacobs body burned to a crisp and now lay just a pile of black ashes.

The man with the hat looked at Martin. "Do it." He said with a low voice. A voice that I had not heard from the man yet.

"Gladly, Master!" Martin yelled as he bent down and scooped with his hands the ashes of the dead Doctor. He began to pour the ashes over the man that was still kneeling and quivering.

Thomas watched with a confused look upon his face while Martin starting cursing at the man that was still in the same position, bowing down before the demon.

Martin finished dumping the ashes on the trembling man. "Master, I would like for you to consider my son, Gerald. He has already been an impressive servant of yours, and I'm sure will take the oath as I have."

Again, the darker and lower voice rumbled through the air. "Yes. Bring him to me as well, and make sure this other one comes to know me."

Martin bowed his head. "Yes, Master."

I stood there and watched as I knew this was only a dream, but a lot of my dreams lately have had some sort of significance and were somehow pertinent to my situation. I wanted to scream out, but something kept from doing so. I had even tried, but my voice was gone.

All I could do was watch as I witnessed what the people needed to be set free from. There was vast darkness that was holding them in the city. I could finally see the dark agenda that was trying to be implemented. I started to see what I was called to do.

Elohim, give me strength. As soon as I even thought that in my head, all of the men looked over at me like they could hear me. My vision went black. Cold, dark silence.

— C —

Dinner was coming to an end as they all talked about the city. It was mostly Mark asking the mayor questions about the inner circle of government. The Mayor mentioned several times that he enjoyed conversing with the young man.

They laughed together and drank their wine. Mellissa even noticing Sarah laughing at times, but she had an uncanny ability to maintain .

Mellissa also payed attention to Sarah's reactions throughout the night. The Mayor's wife seemed to keep to herself as she started to clear the table?. Martin was his loud and boisterous self as he indulged the guests.

"Sarah, can I help you clear the table." Mellissa looked at her while the mayor was telling Mark Jr. and Jordy about growing up under the great James Hurd.

Martin immediately interrupted his story. "She's just fine, Mrs. Waters. Please, you are our guests."

Mellissa looked at Sarah who only smiled. The Mayor continued his story as the widow sat back down in her seat.

She wanted to appear to be enthralled by the conversation, but she was too busy trying to figure Sarah out. She watched as the housewife maintained her composure throughout the course of the night.

How does she do it? What is she really thinking? Is she trained to act like this?

Sarah worked around the kitchen getting everything cleaned up while the others talked.

Mellissa looked at her watch. It was already past 10 pm. "I'm terribly sorry, Mayor Black. I completely lost track of time. We should be going."

Martin looked at Mellissa and smiled. "No worries, my dear. Sarah and I rarely have good company. It's been our pleasure."

— C —

Sarah had listened to her husband ramble on about James Hurd. She was confident that her husband had something to do with his death.

She continued to clean and put things away in the kitchen. The Mayor's wife mostly wanted to avoid being in the other room and listening Martin's hubris.

She made her way back to the table and cleared her husband's dishes from in front of him. She noticed that he didn't even touch the sauce. Her heart sunk as she realizes her plan had failed. *It was a faulty plan at best,* she thought.

She wondered if an opportunity to speak to Mellissa would arise. At least to warn her about the Mayor's plan to brainwash the young Mark Jr. The need to be stealthy and cautious went without saying, but she felt the need to warn the widow.

She wondered if she could slip her a note of some sort. There was always the risk that Mellissa would report the behavior to Martin, but she felt the need to take the opportunity.

Sarah returned to the dining room to hear them getting to leave the Hurd Manor. "Martin, Mellissa? Would either of you like a coffee or tea before you leave?"

Martin looked at his wife. "That's very kind to offer of you, Honey. Yes, Melissa, would you like a coffee?"

"Oh no, that's quite alright. Thank you for your kindness. I never have coffee this late." Mellissa smiled.

Sarah returned her smile though inside her heart sank. She needed to find another way to talk to her. Maybe a note in her blouse pocket as they exchange a hug on the way out. The housewife was conflicted and nervous. *What if he sees me? What if she tells on me? I'm as good as dead anyway. I only hope that she would appreciate the gesture. It's what I would want if Mark were my son.*

She felt the stress of her indecisiveness overwhelming her. *Do I even want this woman as an ally?* Sarah returned to the kitchen and entered the restroom of the side of the breakfast nook. On a single napkin, she wrote the words, "Convince Mark not to join." She folded it and slipped it into the waistline of her skirt under her apron.

She would strategically have to make sure that Martin was on her left side as she tried to slip the note to Mellissa on her right side.

She returned to the dining room, through the kitchen as she saw her guests preparing to leave. Her husband, though on the top of his game, she could tell he was still distracted. Most likely he was bewildered when he received the books. Sarah was also confused as to why her husband wanted them so much. *What is in those books? Why did Mellissa have them?*

Sarah didn't know what to think of the widow. She found herself wondering how Mellissa would do deal with Martin. How would *she* handle such a horrible man?

Was her husband like Martin? He couldn't have been, could he? She wanted someone to trust, but there could be no certainty until she went forward with the note.

The three Waters and the two Blacks made their way to the foyer. Martin was still explaining to Mark what to expect at the second psych evaluation. Sarah remembered overhearing about these second psych evaluations. They were more like seances than an evaluation. It sent chills down Sarah's spine.

Mark offered his hand to the mayor. "Mayor Black, I can't thank you enough for the opportunity and the hospitality tonight. It has been a pleasure to dine with you, and I'm greatly looking forward to working alongside you in the citadel someday."

Martin reached for his hand and pulled him in closer. He placed his left hand on Mark Jr.'s shoulder. "Mark, it's men like you that we need running this city. I am the one privileged to work with such great potential. You're a great man being raised by an extraordinary woman."

Sarah clenched her jaw and closed her eyes as she stood slightly behind Martin. She could hardly take hypocrisy. His duplicity was painful for her to watch. Martin would shake the hands of his people, but behind their backs, he would make a mockery of them.

"And Jordy, don't talk so much next time." He laughed. Jordy politely laughed as well.

Sarah could tell that Mellissa was trying to hurry the process along. "Seriously, thank you both so much for hosting us. Sarah, that duck was incredible."

"I can give you the recipe sometime." Sarah reached in to hug Mellissa. As she did, she slipped the napkin out of her waistline and into Mellissa's pocket.

"That would be appreciated, but I'm sure I won't be able to make it like that." Mellissa returned the hug and also offered her hand for the mayor to shake.

"This was honestly one of the most pleasant evenings." Martin had an enormous smile on his face. Sarah knew she successfully planted the note without her husband's knowledge.

Mark opened the door behind his mother. "Yes, it certainly was!"

— C —

Martin watched as the three of them exited the manor. He thought several times throughout the night that it went a lot better than expected. He sensed no hostile feelings from Mellissa and thought the children were extremely lovely.

She must feel that she can trust us. Why else would she give me the book so freely? This may be the start of a fruitful relationship, he thought as he waved as his guests left the house.

Sarah, next to him, also waving to their neighbors was another pleasant surprise tonight. She was acting as a submissive, textbook Copperline wife should. Martin knew that she was undoubtedly worried about the children, so he already resolved that she could spend the night with them in the attic. Especially, since she couldn't know that he would be headed back out to meet with Tom, and other members of his task force.

Finding that pathetic spec was top priority now that the book had been returned. He would also take a better look at the book himself to see what Mark left behind for people to see.

The door shut and he and his wife remained looking at each other in an awkward silence. "Thank you, Sarah, for a wonderful evening."

She nodded and waited for his next words.

"I have plenty of work to do, which includes reading the notes in that book." He touched her shoulder. "I know you've probably been thinking about the children all night. Why don't you feel free to spend the night up there with them."

He knew that she would still be concerned by the thought of her children bound in their attic, but she would take what he would give her.

"Thank you, Martin."

Martin stood and watched as she quickly went out of his view. He shut a few of the lights off in the downstairs rooms and started heading into the kitchen. He grabbed the books from the counter and took another quick glance inside. He began brewing tea while he studied some of the contents of the books. It didn't appear to make much sense to him and he wondered why Mark held it with such high regard.

He poured his hot tea into a red mug and closed the book. Martin put the book under his arm as he opened the door to the basement and headed down the stairs. At the bottom of the stairs, he turned on a single hanging light. He took a sip of his tea, mostly to mask the scent of his rancid air.

Their house was one of the first ones built in Copperline by James Hurd himself. It was a Victorian-style mansion built on an old stone foundation with a dark red dirt floor. The basement was mostly unoccupied except for the furnace and the hot water boiler, which were modern additions when Martin and Sarah moved in.

Sarah asked earlier tonight about the man living in the basement. The woman became hysterical as she told him that their son was allegedly speaking to whoever it was. He tried to convince her that she was crazy for even thinking such a thing, but Martin wondered why he, himself couldn't communicate like that to the great spirit. Martin convinced her to take half of a Xanax.

He looked around the area, but there was no sign of the beast. He would never let Sarah know details regarding Asmodeus.

Martin walked to the corner of the basement where he moved an old wooden door that was leaning against the wall. He entered a stone hallway with old cobblestone stairs that led deeper and deeper into the ground.

Only lit by a small keyring flashlight, Martin made his way down the staircase until he came to another small steel access door. He entered his passcode and opened it.

Martin crouched his tall frame through the tiny steel door and found himself in the far end of the city's subway.

He listened the sound of his shoes echoing through the empty chamber as he walked. Illuminated by faint ceiling lights every 12 feet. He counted the light fixtures out of habit as he trudged on toward the hospital.

However, tonight he needed to focus on the task at hand. The spec was somewhere in his city. Between his disappearing act and the sudden appearing of the book, he was quite distracted during the evening.

After quite some time walking, he approached a door and a passcode monitor. Martin entered the code and the door opened that led him into the bottom floor and basement of the hospital. Only third shift nurses and emergency medics were working that time of night.

He made his way to the elevator and went to the lab where Dr. Jacobs' body still remained. He would take care of the body and discuss plans with his brother.

Entering the containment lab, he found his brother already there standing over the lifeless body of David Jacobs.

Tom stood with his hand on his chin. "I guess, you taught him a lesson?" Tom shook his head.

Martin looked at Tom and then the body. "I would do the same thing to you if you become as incompetent as he did."

Seventeen

Mellissa arrived back at home and entered the house with her children. "Mark, that was lovely wasn't it."

He nodded. "Now to pass tomorrow."

"You just have to believe the truth." Mellissa tapped her finger on his forehead and whispered, "What do you know as true? You found a banned book and handed it to your mother to turn it into the Mayor. You did the right thing, Son."

Jordy had already made her way into her room to change and get ready for bed.

Mark looked nervous. "But mother, what about…"

"About what, honey? That's all you saw." She looked into his eyes. "I just need you to say it. Don't identify with what you think you saw, Mark."

Mark hung his head. He knew what she was doing. His father used to tell them ways to pass a polygraph. He used to tell them if they can pass a poly, they could pass the serum.

"Yes, ma'am." Mark's voice was quiet.

"Mark." She gently grabbed his chin. "I need you to hear yourself say it."

Mark fixed his posture and spoke with confidence. "I found the book among my father's things that my mother had forgotten about. I gave it to her as it was an unapproved book. She said she would turn it into the mayor immediately."

Mellissa patted his shoulder. "Good man. Now, just watch yourself say it in the mirror. You're a fine protector of this family, son."

She watched as he Mark walked away and headed to his bedroom. She loved how much he reminded her of her husband. The widow sighed as she went into her bedroom.

She started to take off her blouse when something fell out of her pocket. It appeared to be a napkin. Bending down to pick it up, she set it on her dresser.

That's strange, she thought. *How did that get in there?* Mellissa put a t-shirt on and grabbed the napkin as she made her way downstairs into the kitchen.

The trash can sat beside the refrigerator where she tossed the napkin without thinking any more of the peculiarity of it winding up in her pocket.

She took a look at several of the papers that her husband left behind. She wondered if there were cameras watching her. The thought of that disgusted her, but to be safe, she put the pages that her husband left behind into the book she was reading.

I'm not going to take any chances, Mellissa thought. From a distance, it would appear that she was only reading a novel before bed, but in actuality, she studied many of the notes with their wealth of information.

There was one note that stuck out to her. It looked as if it was a minimized photocopy of a donor certificate from the date when

Mark was born. She read it twice. *Mark was right. He had a twin, and somewhere in this city was her other child.*

A flood of emotion came over her. Her breathing became labored as she tried to keep in the tears. She held her hand over her heart that pounded vigorously in the woman's chest.

She touched the part of the document that read, "Male. Donor, M. Waters." She would've gone her whole life and never had known if it weren't for her husband. However, she found her emotions evolving into anger. *The Mayor has my child. I need...*

A soft knock on her door startled her. Mellissa shut the book and dried her eyes. "Come in!"

Jordy entered. Her eyes were red and makeup had run from the tears. "I miss him, mom." She collapsed into her mother's open arms.

"I know, Honey. So do I. It'll take an eternity to not miss him." Mellissa brushed her daughter's hair as she curled up against her.

"But you are so strong. I watched you all night at the mayor's house." Jordy lifted her sleeve to dry her eyes.

"You may see that on the outside, but on the inside I'm lost without your father. When I'm by myself, I cry an infinite amount of tears for that man, and I'll cry an infinite more still. Your father was the greatest man I have ever met."

Mellissa's eyes were watering again. She looked at her hand stroking her daughter's hair.

"You and I must be strong, Jordy. This city is not for the faint of heart. It's a threshing floor that will separate the ones who least expect it. They won't take mercy on the grievers. We must stick together and never be swerved."

"I'll miss most, the times that he would teach me to never stop dreaming of a world outside Copperline," Jordy said.

"I'll miss that too, Honey." Mellissa loved that she and her daughter were connecting. She hadn't had too many times like this before Mark passed. Jordy was in every definition of the word, a daddy's girl. "We have always been so proud of our children. You'll take your talents and abilities wherever you want. Don't settle for just Copperline."

Jordy looked at her mother. "Do you think…"

"I think that when the time is right, and we are all on board, we could move wherever you wanted." Mellissa smiled as she spoke to Jordy. If it was only assurance that Jordy needed, then assurance is what Mellissa would giver her. However, she wanted to run from this city. The fact that Jordy was even head-faking in that direction was music to her ears.

Mellissa's biggest concern was now, her sons. One which was about to embark upon a dangerous journey with a bunch of people that wouldn't think twice about eating him alive, and the other was somewhere inside the city and may not even know she existed.

She wondered what he looked like. *Was he an identical twin? Did Mark know him? Why wouldn't he tell me.* She may have even forced her husband into a situation that could've gotten him killed if he confessed. She was sure more than ever that her husband's death wasn't accidental.

If the mayor was messing with people's lives, to the point of taking children and killing people, she would find a way to expose the lies. Mark in many ways held this family on his shoulders, but now she was placed as the protector and provider.

Suddenly, the shrill sound of her phone startled her. Her eyes widened immediately and her heart jumped out of her chest. She expected to hear another ring from the phone, but it quickly became silent. Mellissa stood to her feet and listened. She felt the softness of the carpet as the woman stepped into the hallway to try to hear, but it was quiet. She noticed Mark's door was shut, but she could see the light on under the door.

She crept closer to the door, one footstep at a time. The closer she got to the door, she could make out Mark talking softly into the phone. It sounded as if he was arguing with someone.

She pressed her ear up against the wooden door, but the sound of muffled talking dissipated. She rested her hand on the doorknob when she felt it slowly turn.

She quickly backed herself up and stood there in front of the door. She wondered how she would explain herself, but then realized her son was the one that needed to explain.

"Mother?" He asked.

"Were you talking to someone?" She stood there looking concerned.

"Yes, but…" He paused. She could tell he was nervous.

"But what, Son?" She asked.

"Do you trust me?" He asked as he held out a piece of paper that he had taken from his mother's pile. The paper looked like one that had the spec information on it.

"Son, of course, I trust you, but…"

Mark held his finger up to his lips and shook his head. "No. Mother, please just answer yes or no. Do you trust me?"

She paused for what seemed like an eternity. *What is he up to?* She saw a sense of passion in him that her husband had. She always trusted him, which is why they stayed in Copperline all this time. She was also afraid for him. This was her baby boy.

Do I actually trust him? Mellissa asked herself. She felt that she only had one logical answer to give her son.

"Yes." She sighed. "Yes, Mark. I trust you."

— C —

Martin and X reviewed the video feed until they lost track of the spec after he exited the hospital building. None of them could figure out how they lost track of it so easily.

Martin made every guard aware of what the spec was wearing, and what it looked like. The spec was described as a 5' 10" Caucasian male with light brown hair, and blueish green eyes. It hadn't shaved in three days, so it should be a little easier to spot since it wasn't a season approved for facial hair.

Tom looked over the books while Martin focused on the camera feeds. He noticed that the notes were inconsistent with the subject matter on each page. *There's got to me more somewhere.*

"There's no way that this is all here." Tom tapped Martin on the shoulder with the book.

"Why do you mean?" Martin stayed glued to the screen.

Tom cleared his throat. "The notes in the headers and footers don't even come close to matching the notes in the margins. Some notes were used with black ink that looks like it was from a ballpoint pen, while the header and footer notes look as if they were done with a gel type pen." He paused for a brief second. "Also, other notes were written with the pressure that left ghostwriting on the next page. The header and footer notes did not. While the handwriting is very similar, the header and footer notes have lowercase letters, while the other notes are all caps."

"Tom, it was probably written at different points in time. People's writing changes." Martin was still glued to the surveillance monitors. "Give me something good."

"The margin notes are pertinent to the subject matter with some sort of correlating code, which I'm assuming is from Mark's time in the military. The header and footer notes seem like they are just random musings. Someone is either trying to throw us off or this is really impressive code." Tom looked at X. "If it's the latter, it's a shame you killed him. He could've been quite useful to us."

Martin looked up from the monitor for the first time "Tom, you will refrain from to talking to my son like that." Martin looked at him out of the corner of his eye. Tom knew exactly what this meant, so he had to counteract.

Tom put his finger right in Martin's chest. "You may have been given more power, but you know as well as anybody that you need my intelligence." Tom grinned, which he knew would irritate his brother. He needed Tom.

Tom removed his finger and continued. "As I was saying. I think it's a combination of someone messing with us and the real notes. Maybe his son, his wife, the spec. Do we even know how many people had this before us? No. So we have to assume, his family took the information they needed and threw us a bone."

Martin was still looking at Tom through the corner of his eye. "Regardless Tom, we have the boy. We will have his mind tomorrow on a platter to pick apart. His vulnerable mind is no match for the truth serum. If we wanted to, we could brainwash that boy and have him turn on his mother. A tiny little woman and her pathetic mute daughter is no match for this mayor!"

"Gentlemen." X interrupted the two brothers. "Look at this."

Both men viewed the monitor. A still image that X found of a man matching the spec's description headed into the treeline by the old founder's path.

"Send the closest sector guards." Martin's face was distorted into a frown that even X was not familiar with. "Demand them to bring it to me alive. I want to be the one to kill it."

— C —

I was startled by a rustling sound in the woods behind me. I jolted awake by a snapping sound. I listened intently. *What was that? Could they have found me already?*

Having no idea what time it was, I looked at the clear night sky and saw that the moon had moved considerably. I must've slept for hours. It'll be morning soon enough, but I needed to get better cover.

I looked for any sign of light, but nothing. If they did find me using surveillance, all they would've seen was me headed into the tree line. There was still a million places I could've run in here. It would still take them hours to find me, especially without light. I at least tried to lie to convince myself of these things.

If they were smart, they would search without lights anyway. Lights would obviously give away their location and show me where they were.

If there was one thing I knew about this mayor, he would do anything to keep this kind of activity quiet. Less noise equaled fewer problems. That would be to my advantage. While these men were trained to guard the people of Copperline, they weren't exactly trained to hunt.

The spec life meant always maneuvering in the dark. We rarely had the use of light. Whenever we saw a light, it meant a guard or a nurse was coming to torment us somehow. A light meant we had to make a choice to be seen or to hide.

I would not go back. I had burned that bridge and though the path ahead of me was uncertain, I was sure that I would not end up back in that hospital.

I listened closely. Another snap. This time, I knew it had to be something of substantial size. Copperline didn't have wild animals or domesticated animals for that matter. I sat up slowly. I didn't want to move until I absolutely had to. If I made a sudden and stupid move, they could see me first and then I'd be done. I had no knowledge of where I was, or where I'd go.

I wondered about the tree that I fell into just a few days ago. I was almost certain that it was located on the other side of the city.

This side was definitely more grassland. The other was more like a deciduous forest.

I became very conscious of my breathing. I was amazed at how loud everything became in the stillness of nature. I felt as if my breathing was the only thing I could hear other than the snap sounds coming from somewhere in the woods behind me.

Another snap. This time I started to panic. The sound was coming from behind me to my left. I turned my head slowly to see if I could see anything out of the corner of my eye, but all I could make out was brush and small trees with larger red pines every 5 to 8 feet apart. However, I fixed my eyes on the area that I felt the sound was coming from. If I kept my eyes there. Any sudden movement would give it away.

Snap! Another startling sound, but this time it came from my right side.

My heart rate increased instantly. My breathing was deafening in between the sudden sounds coming from the forest.

Then I saw something. It was a silhouette of a body walking toward me on the beaten walking path that I followed last night. I could see the figure out of the corner of my right eye. The walker must've been about 60 or 70 yards away. It was closing in faster than a walking pace.

I wondered what I should do, but I was paralyzed by my fear. *Should I run now, or should I wait and see if they go past me?*

I strained my eyes to see the figure. It looked like they were jogging toward me.

They must see me now. I have no other choice. I need to run. I need to move now if I'm going to get away.

I waited a few more seconds. I looked around to see if there were any obstacles that I could hide behind as I made my getaway.

Snap! This sound came from my left again in the direction of the woods. There were more than one. I started panicking. I was trapped. *No. I will not go back.*

"Hold it right there!" A voice shouted from my left. The man yelling sounded so close that I was surprised that I couldn't see them.

I hung my head and cursed.

To be continued...

About The Author

Peter Michael Talbot is a pastor and teacher who started writing novels as a promise to his students. Talbot enjoys writing about spiritual truths that transcend religious ideologies. He likes to think of them as modern-day parables. Peter and his wife, Bethany reside in Maine with their three boys (one on the way).

www.ingramcontent.com/pod-product-compliance
Lightning Source LLC
Chambersburg PA
CBHW030108100526
44591CB00009B/331